RELIGION AND SCIENCE

RELIGION AND SCIENCE

An Exploration of Some Problems in Science and Religion

EDWARD W. H. VICK

Energion Publications
Gonzalez, Florida
2019

Copyright © 1975, Edward W. H. Vick

ISBN10: 1-63199-618-5
ISBN13: 978-1-63199-618-4

Energion Publications
P. O. Box 841
Gonzalez, FL 32560

energion.com
pubs@energion.com

Original publication 1975 by Epworth Press. Reprint Edition

TO ESTHER

Contents

	Author's Note	7
1	Different Kinds of Question	9
2	Conflict	16
3	Fact and Proof	23
4	The Scientist and His Facts	32
5	Subject and Object	40
6	What is Possible?	48
7	Miracles	53
8	What is Nonsense?	63
9	What is Religion?	69
10	Interaction	78
11	Science and the Future	85
12	Religion and the Future	91
13	The Question about Beginnings	99
14	Revelation	106
15	Faith	112
16	The Pattern of the World	118
	Index	127

Author's Note

WHAT is written in these chapters is supposed to be interesting and sensible but not complicated. It is hoped that people of differing interests will find it helpful in opening up issues and clarifying important questions. I could hope that it would fall into the hands of people who are indifferent and who would be prompted to discussion by a teacher or by the leader of a group, and begin a new quest.

It is based on the conviction that religious questions can be presented in a non-partisan manner. That does not mean with a neutral kind of impartiality. To be impartial does not mean that we have no bias. It means that we recognize what it is and that we allow for it. To be able to discuss religion impartially means that you don't have to be worried all the time that you will end up believing, or that you have not made the other person believe yet! You don't have to be committed to discuss the issues. Just interested, even a little.

When one hopes that his writing will be popular, I suppose one means that it will be readable by the non-specialist. At least that's what I mean.

EDWARD W. H. VICK

Nottingham 1974

1 | Different Kinds of Question

THERE are different ways of explaining things.

You are on the bus going in the direction of the city. A friend sees you and shouts, 'Why are you going to town?' To this you reply, 'Because I'm on the bus!' To which you get the answer, 'Don't be funny. Answer my question!' But, in a sense, you did answer the question. You did not give the answer that was expected and that is why the question was thrown back at you. What you did was to state a cause for your going to town. So let's try again. 'Why are you going to town?' 'Because I'm meeting Jim. Because I'm going to the ice show with him.' But if the questioner persists you will have to say, 'I'm going because I want to go. I decided to go. It is my will to go. And that's all there is to say.' Of course there is another answer which most people would never think of, let alone give. But some religious persons would: 'Because it is the will of God.'

Let's take another case.

A child died after contracting an unusual disease. So you ask the parents, 'Why did Jimmy die?' To which they might give one or more of the following answers: 'Because his body did not have the resistance it took to fight the infection.' 'Because we took him on safari with us, instead of leaving him with his granny.' 'Because it was the will of God.' We could understand quite well what the parents meant with either of the first two answers. Those are quite acceptable although they do point to different facts. In the first case to a set of physical ones, in the second to a decision that was taken. There are people who would give the third, but we would probably find this difficult to get hold of, as indeed we did in the first example.

It is late afternoon in the Lake District. Someone is watching the sunset. Suppose you intrude upon him and ask the question,

Different Kinds of Question

'What's happening?' You might get a lesson in optics: light of different wavelengths is striking the retina which in turn gives rise to a stimulation of the visual lobes of the brain, so I get a sensation which I register to you as *seeing the sunset*. The phrase is a sort of shorthand for all this complicated activity. That would be an answer to the question. Appropriate in a physics lesson, but acceptable, and understandable as an explanation. You might get the answer that recounts his experiencing of beauty. Indeed he might say, 'Hush now. I'll tell you later.' Later he explains that the sight of the sinking sun had stirred feelings within him, and that he was responding to the beauty of the scene. That too is an explanation. This time it is an explanation in terms of aesthetics. But you might get a third answer—the religious answer. 'The heavens declare the glory of God and the firmament showeth his handiwork.' The sun has been an object of worship for ages.

In each of these cases one level does not exclude or make impossible the others. It is incomplete in itself. It does not cover the whole ground. There is more to be said. What we have to do then is to ask what ground it does cover, if any. There will seem to us to be answers which do not say anything. But we must be careful not to dismiss these as simply nonsense. They may in the future come to have some meaning. Nor must we think that one sort of answer will say everything. Take one further example.

Why does the play *Hamlet* end in tragedy? 'Because Hamlet killed Polonius and this led to a train of events, and so to the tragic end.' 'Because Hamlet was both irresolute and impulsive.' 'Because it was God's will: "There's a divinity that shapes our ends, rough-hew them how we will!"' Now each of these could be argued plausibly—the last less. It is the consequence of a way of seeing rather than a way of arguing. It is an explanation which Hamlet finds plausible.

These several examples make it clear that explanation can be given *on different levels*. We can give an account of the causes, on the assumption that effects are produced by causes. Since the effects are predictable when the causes are known, to detail the causes is, in a sense, to give an explanation of the effect. But if these are made to cover the whole ground, we are left with the feeling that such an explanation is not really satisfactory. People on buses do end up where buses end up. Children with low resistance do succumb to germs. People watching sunsets do have their optic nerves stimulated. The killing of Polonius did have immediate repercussions. But more will have to be said in each case to satisfy us.

Causes are not reasons. We feel a need to supplement the causal account, however elaborate and accurate it might be, by a further explanation. So the second kind of answer given in our illustrations has to do with the will of the agent, or agents, concerned. The optical explanation of the person watching the sunset would do just as well if he were watching the emptying of dustbins. The physical explanation would cover the death of a dog as well as the death of Jimmy. And the 'Because I'm on the bus' answer strikes us as amusing because it does not seem to explain anything at all. In each case the result has to do with the person, a living, willing, being. In any adequate account his personality and his will must be taken into account.

Scientific explanation on the causal level is *deliberately* selective. It does not cover the whole ground. Will as a factor may not be accounted for. But in a comprehensive explanation it must be taken into account. The ballistics expert plays an important part, perhaps sometimes a decisive part, in the criminal investigation. But there's a lot more beside the account of the matter which he's able to explain in his way. You have to ask questions about the person of the criminal.

Now religious people go on to say that the will of God is a factor which should not be forgotten. They have the persistent habit of saying *whatever happens* or happened is or was the will of God. That seems to be a very strange way of accounting for it, since the statement is made to include everything, and not just the particular matter in question. This does not mean that believers do not distinguish between important and decisive moments in which they see the will of God in a special way from other occasions. They do.

Please notice that the religious explanation is not a substitute for the other kinds of explanation. The scientist does not say, if he happens also to be a believer: 'Since I can't find an adequate cause-effect explanation I'll just have to say that God causes it that way.' In an earlier, less scientific time, this was what might sometimes be said. God became the 'God of the gaps'. When the project ran

Different Kinds of Question

into difficulties, or when there was an area which had not yet been scientifically explained (in terms of causes and effects) there, it was thought, the God-explanation could be employed. Theologians learned slowly that that kind of God was not worth having. He would become less and less relevant as science closed one gap after another. One can't go on fighting rear-guard actions for ever. Now the scientist says, 'I do not yet know, but hope with due diligence that we can pass from ignorance to knowledge.'

Our point is that the three levels of explanation need not conflict. Determinism on the causal level, Freedom on the voluntary level, and Will of God are not incompatible. You could 'explain' everything on the level of physical causes and not have touched the problem of freedom. Freedom cannot be analysed in the categories of physics.

There is another sense in which a question can be taken in different ways, and different kinds of answer be given to it. The different sciences have their own ways of answering questions. This is what distinguishes them from each other. The task of learning a science involves the understanding of the language and the methods it uses. Take a question such as 'What is man?' and from different disciplines we shall get different kinds of answer.

The biologist might answer this question by speaking of the size and activity of the brain and explaining its physical functions. The psychologist might answer in terms of man's intelligence and the distinction between that and the intelligence of the higher animals. A philosopher might answer by speaking of his conscience as making him distinctive. The theologian would speak of spirit, of faith, and of man as the creature of God.

Other examples could be given of questions which might be answered on different levels. Think of some.

This brief introduction will be complete if we make three points:

1. Where it is a case of questions which can be answered on different levels it will help if we are aware of the differences between the possible answers so that we do not confuse one kind with another. If we distinguish the levels from one another, we may see that some levels of answer are much more important than others.

2. On each level there are good and bad ways of answering the question. In the above example, concerning man, there are recog-

Religion and Science

nized procedures for discussing the question from within the different disciplines. If we are attempting to answer (or to understand) the question from a particular point of view and with a particular method, we must be acquainted with the ways of tackling it which are recognized within the particular discipline.

3. One kind of answer need not exclude another kind of answer. It is a popular, and sometimes welcomed, mistake to think that if some science can answer the question asked, then there is no further word to be spoken about it. This is one of the ways of taking a short cut in discussing the relations between science and religion. If science does not find evidence for the believer's claim that man is the creature of God, the question is not worth pursuing any further. That is how it's seen (sometimes) from one side. If science does not bear out the claims that God is the creator, then so much the worse for science. That's how it's seen (sometimes) from the other side. Both are wrong. It's not a matter of either/or, but rather of both/and.

This makes it much more difficult and taxing. But it also makes it possible to be a cultured believer on the one hand, and an unprejudiced unbeliever on the other. It is not necessary to be a scientist in order to see issues involved in the discussion of relations between science and religion. You have to be intelligent and you have to be serious. The other mistake dies harder. You do not have to be committed to a particular faith in order to understand something about religion. There are ways of talking about religion which are not concerned to 'witness' to you nor to persuade you to be a believer. You can go a long way in understanding what religion is, and what it is not, simply by having a look at what is available generally: in books about religion, in the newspapers, on the radio. You will find that there are people who will be helpful in explaining to you what religion is about, without wanting to persuade you to have faith or to join a religious body. That may or may not come later. What is important for us now is to look reasonably at some of the problems of particular interest to those of us who wish to be well-informed about both science and religion and would welcome the discovery of some kind of working relationship between them.

We now raise a question which will be in the minds of most people when any discussion of religion takes place, the question of God. It is not easy to talk about God. God is the theologian's *problem*. That is important. It is his problem to make discourse about God intelligible. Is there a level upon which such discourse is meaningful? Apart from oaths and clauses in insurance companies' forms ('act of God') where the function of the words is quite plain we might clear the ground by indicating where such language is *not* meaningful, that is where it does not clarify or explain anything. This will remove part of the difficulty. It's hard enough to talk about God. We need not make it harder by raising useless problems, or by introducing needless difficulties, one of which is that of oversimplifying the difficulties, either in a negative or a positive direction.

Specifically, shall the theologian talk about God in the language of *will* as was done briefly in this chapter, that is in the language of human experience? Or shall he refuse to apply to God such analogies drawn from human experience and, so to speak, put a minus sign in front of all such human characteristics when speaking of God?

Indeed, why speak about God at all?

No one knows more about the difficulties of God-language than does the person who seriously tries to use it and to specify the level of discourse on which it is appropriately used, differentiating that from other levels where other sorts of language are appropriate.

Summary and Conclusion

Questions can be answered on different levels, which levels have rules of right discourse and which need not necessarily conflict with one another. Is there any level of discourse upon which God-language is helpful?

Discussion Questions

Take the following questions and propose different *kinds* of possible answer. Then ask what *kinds* of answer you have given.

What is life?

What is death?

Religion and Science

What is man?

What happened at Dunkirk?

Why should I refrain from murder? stealing?

Why did Captain Scott and his companions die? Yan Palach?

2 | Conflict

CONFLICTS occur in different ways and on different levels. Not every argument or disagreement is of the same kind, to be settled in the same way. If we assume a willingness to explore and to question, and the openness to consider what before we simply had not held before our attention, we might be in for some surprises. We shall hardly be able to escape revising our opinions.

Conflict occurs when two people disagree in their claims to truth. Notice three levels on which conflict can occur:

1. When one person says that a particular proposition is true, and someone else claims that a contradictory, or an apparently contradictory proposition is true. We could call it a 'This is true, no it isn't' kind of conflict.

2. When one party makes certain assumptions about things which he says are necessary if we are going to think properly, and another makes different ones. Different perspectives, or ways of looking, will produce different spectacles. What we see will depend on how we look. Different people look at the same (?) things in different ways. What they see is different. They may come to think that their way of looking and the assumptions through which they see are the right ones; we may do likewise about our way of looking and our assumptions. It is superficial then to argue about the facts which we believe that we see. The conflict is here upon a more fundamental level. So, for example, if one party were to think on the assumption 'anything religious is superstitious', and another on the assumption 'whatever the Christian religion says is true', there would soon be an inevitable clash.

3. When a set of assumptions and methods for understanding are developed and co-ordinated systematically, people who work with them may come to feel that their science (for that is the name we give to such systematic ways of knowing) provides the only

valid avenue to what is worth knowing. (Note that we are using the term science in a broad sense, like the German *Wissenschaft*. So it includes the social sciences, history, psychology.) Conflict can take place when such sets of perspectives and attitudes come into contact.

Conflict is resolved in different ways. Obviously, since there are different ways of having an argument, there are different ways of settling it. It may be that in certain instances it is better to keep on disputing. Doubt and discussion is a most important stimulus to the discovery of truth. But there must be a willingness to explore from both sides. It takes two to make a quarrel. So different kinds of people have different kinds of things to learn when a division of opinion is freely expressed in debate.

We suggest three ways in which conflict might be resolved.

1. One side might show the other to be wrong.

The most common case of this is when someone has not got all the facts that he should have at his command and is arguing that something is so, only to be corrected when someone better informed brings out something that he has overlooked. (You say Mary Smith is trustworthy. Have you not read of her stretch at Borstal?) One who is in a better position to know the facts is in a better position to state the 'case'.

Another kind of case of disagreement is where one has failed to reason correctly. Teachers of mathematics and of logic (and other subjects) are out to see that the process of reasoning is correct in any given instance. Whatever the subject of discourse, if we make false logical moves, we are bound to end in error, or alternatively reach the truth by accident!

2. Both sides might acknowledge the scope of their methods of arriving at truth, come to recognize (as perhaps they had not done before) the legitimate demands about the limitations of their methods, and recognize the scope for the proper application of the methods of the other party.

3. Two parties holding certain assumptions, looking at reality from different perspectives, may come to see that when their apparently incompatible perspectives are seen more comprehensively within a wider context, they illuminate rather than contradict one another. In a case like this, it may be necessary for a third party to enter the discussion and show to both that there is a

more encompassing perspective within which the two may be set. Resolving a conflict is thus sometimes a matter of understanding a language, of communicating, where before there was a failure to get it across, or to get it through.

What we have said has oversimplified the matter. An important argument has many facets, and in conducting it one is fighting on many fronts at the same time. But it will help, I believe, to clear away some elementary objections. It may help to show that some objections are not half serious enough. For, if one is going to be serious about the business of having a discussion, one must simply discuss. It will not do simply to pontificate.

The classic example of such conflict took place at the dawn of our modern era when Copernicus and Galileo, the latter with more fact, instruments, mathematics and theory at his command than the former, insisted that not the earth but the sun was the central point of the universe. The opposition to such a far-reaching innovation was practically unanimous. In the name of theology, of philosophy, of church doctrine and of the Bible the new idea was roundly condemned. So sure were the churchmen of their position and of course of the implications of the position that opposed it that they refused to look through Galileo's telescope. Religious leaders who on other issues fought each other tooth and nail were one in their opposition to the new astronomy, as the following statements show. The former is from the Catholic side. The other is from Luther.

'The first proposition that the sun is the centre and does not revolve about the earth, is foolish, absurd, false in theology, and heretical, because expressly contrary to Holy Scripture.... The second proposition, that the earth is not the centre, but revolves about the sun is absurd, false in philosophy, and, from a theological point of view at least, opposed to the true faith.'

'People give ear to an upstart astrologer who strove to show that the earth revolves, not the heavens or the firmament, the sun and the moon. Whoever wishes to appear must devise some new system, which of all systems is of course the very best. This fool wishes to reverse the entire science of astronomy; but sacred Scripture tells us that Joshua commanded the sun to stand still, and not the earth.'

The course and issue of this particular conflict illustrates our first category, namely, conflict which is due to ignorance of facts is resolved by learning the facts. The Aristotelians and Ptolemaists were shown to be wrong because they had not taken account of what could be shown to be fact. When the facts were known the older 'science' had to give way. Necessary adjustments in theology and philosophy had to be made. This was because the theologians had assumed the factual truth of Aristotle and Ptolemy.

Our second category (Solve the problem of conflict by accepting the legitimacy of different kinds of approach) is illustrated by raising the question of beginnings (How did things begin?) and of endings (How will things end?). There are different *kinds* of answer for these questions. Conflict is inevitable if the biologist and the theologian, or the astronomer and the theologian claim that the different things they say are on the same level of discourse. There need be no conflict if the levels of discourse are clearly differentiated. Since we shall try to show this to be the case in later chapters[1] we shall no longer pursue the matter at this point.

The third category (Solve the problem of conflict by seeing that different perspectives complement rather than conflict with one another) may be briefly illustrated by mentioning that there are different ways of studying the phenomenon of religion. It can be approached as a social phenomenon, as data for the sociologist, or as providing 'psychological fact'. In neither case will the question of the truth of what is believed *necessarily* be raised. This may seem to pose a threat to a convinced believer and smack of agnosticism or atheism. At the least it demands neutrality. We must be ready to see that those who pursue truth in their ways are our allies in our particular quest for truth. They may be working in a different room from ours. But truth is always compatible with truth. It is both a hope and a quest that it can be seen to be so.

The development of a comprehensive perspective (compare our fourth category) will make it possible to see the truth and the relative contribution each approach has to make in the quest. The comprehensive perspective will be the reflection of a fundamental attitude. How this is achieved and evaluated will be discussed later.

4. Now there are instances of people knowing the same facts, knowing, let us say, *all* the facts there are to know in the parti-

[1] Chapters 11–13.

cular case, and still disagreeing. For example in a court case. Here what must be decided is whether the prisoner is guilty or not guilty. Let's say both defence and prosecution know the same facts. They draw different conclusions from the same facts. Moreover they try to persuade the jury that theirs is the right conclusion.

The way this is done is by relating facts to facts in a manner that is illuminating, and by letting the reasonableness of the case rest with the impact which that interpretation makes. In such a case we have what has been called a 'non-scientific hypothesis' which explains the facts. But the people who hear the case have to make a decision. We then talk appropriately about conviction. Before the prisoner is convicted the jury is convinced. They make their decision, that the facts are interpreted aright by one or the other of the lawyers.

When the data is the world (= everything that is) then, since there are no more facts to get, it is not a question of getting more facts. It is a question of interpreting the facts that are available. When we have settled the question concerning the proper levels of discourse and the appropriate questions to be discussed on those levels, and of the relations between the different conclusions, sorted things out, so to say, we still have the decision to make. What of the whole lot? If it is really the whole lot then what is called for is the right sort of considerations which will enable us to connect up the facts that we know in the most appropriate manner. We shall then be down to the question of our fundamental attitudes (see Chapter 16).

We shall not be able to do this unless the preliminary problems of what belongs where and who speaks rightly about what are to some extent clarified.

We must make quite sure on the one hand that the version of faith and theology that is up for consideration is an adequate one. This will mean that we shall have to go right to the primary and genuine sources of information, and not simply rest with what might well be a version of the matter which no intelligent and active believer would endorse. This will be true also on the other hand of science. It is very easy to get distorted ideas of what science is doing. Patience will be needed, and openness. We will assume that it is a most worth-while discussion, because something is at stake—truth and authenticity. This is what will make it interesting. We

Religion and Science

will not simply assume from the outset that the quesion is a settled one. 'Oh! Science is about fact, and religion has to do with feeling! What's the point of discussion?' 'Religion has its own avenue to knowledge. We know the truth. What's the point of discussion?' It's the clause, 'What's the point of discussion?' (= there is no point of discussion) that will bring down the blinds. If we are going to have fruitful talk we shall have to avoid such Shut up! clauses.

It is often not realized that the believer is very anxious to repudiate the mistakes and the prejudices of the past, that he has, if he has some intelligence and has given the matter thought, already done so. It is seldom realized by the man in the street how great have been the changes that have taken place in the thinking of the believer during the last century. The believer will be most willing to discuss if he is concerned about truth. So also will the scientist and the scientifically inclined.

Summary and Conclusion

Clarity and understanding result from recognizing the level of discussion and the appropriate arguments to be deployed on the particular level. Conflicts are resolved in different ways. With the resolution of particular conflicts of science and religion, the question of our fundamental attitudes to the world is raised.

Discussion Questions

Why might people disagree about the following? Where would discussion be profitable and where would it be impossible?

That was good value for money.

The French Revolution was a disaster.

Sociology is an interesting subject.

Mr Brown was to blame for the accident.

That is a very large building.

Conflict

This is the correct answer to the mathematical problem.

Miracles do not happen.

Evolution is wrong because the Bible says that God is the Creator.

Psychology is dangerous.

Read the following passages and discuss the problems involved.

God, to the theist, while being the cause of everything, is in the scientific sense the explanation of nothing.

Neither theological nor scientific interests are purely 'practical'; both are human enterprises involving the unquenchable human thirst for *intelligibility*. It is, indeed, this thirst, this desire for understanding, that represents the main area of overlap between science and religion—the overlap that has made possible all those unfortunate battles between them. The battles may be unfortunate, I should add, but the overlap is not; it is what also makes possible our hope for an eventual unification of the human consciousness.

Modern astro-physics, geography, and geology have once for all destroyed the view of the world characteristic of antiquity and the Bible. The conflict of orthodoxy with modern science, which is still carried on here and there, means nothing more from the standpoint of Christian faith than a superfluous protraction of unworthy apologetic devices which viewed as a whole now lies behind us.... By its undreamed of progress science has forced faith to disencumber itself of certain relics of (primitive) science.

Science ... could have developed only in a cultural environment which understood that the world and all that it contains was created by the will and the wisdom of God.

No reason can be given for the nature of God, because that nature is the ground of rationality.

3 | *Fact and Proof*

IT IS a commonly held opinion that science deals with facts and proofs and, for this reason rests, upon the solid ground, that science is somehow more reliable and authoritative than other realms of human experience and creation, especially art and religion. With this in mind we shall take a look at what the scientist does and ask what function proof performs in his work.

Science is methodical exploration. The more advanced the science the more clearly it can specify the principles of its method. In the different sciences appropriate procedures are employed in relation to the data being considered. There is no scientific method as such. Scientific method is to be defined in relation to a particular area of investigation, which gets mapped out more and more clearly as that science develops. Indeed the process of clarifying its procedures *is* the development of that science. A science comes into its own as it clarifies its methods of investigation in relationship to the area of experience being investigated.

The investigator begins by choosing an area of 'nature' or 'experience' to investigate. He isolates the data he will examine, choosing to investigate these rather than others. The various sciences are differentiated from one another by having different data upon which to work and by their different methods in relation to the selected data. There is a two-way traffic between method and data. So physics, chemistry, psychology, history and sociology differ from one another. They are also distinct from philosophy, which might be considered the parent enterprise, from which they broke off in the course of their development. It is in this differentiation from philosophy and from other scientific activity that one and the other can establish themselves as separate sciences. 'We do not enlarge but disfigure sciences, if we allow them to trespass upon one another's territory' (Kant).

Fact and Proof

For example, in the development of the science of psychology the recognition and definition of 'psychological facts' had to be established before the discipline could be differentiated from philosophy, its parent. This involved the staking of the claim that there were ways of observing and explaining man which were distinctive and 'scientific'. The existence of 'schools' of psychology is evidence that the process is not yet complete.

To assemble data, and to provide explanation (=to solve a problem) are the two fundamental motions going on at the same time in a progressive science. Explanation is essentially a process of relating: facts to facts, facts to problems, and problems to facts. In some sciences, the physical sciences, two important principles which are not derived from experience but not unrelated to experience, are fundamental.

1. Observation must be controlled to yield results. You can observe facts until the end of your life and not see anything significant. It is an illusion that physical science deals with facts and facts only! The control of the observation of the facts is effected along two lines: the scientist takes a piece of nature and observes that bit, excluding everything else for the time. There is of course much more that he could have observed, and may, on another occasion observe. But not now. He does *not* take an interest in *all* the phenomena that might be known about the object of his investigation at the moment. If he is interested in the life-expectancy of the human male, he may not be interested in patterns of secretion in the salivary glands. The second aspect of control of observation is that in preparation for an experiment or a series of experiments, he is deliberately *setting up* the conditions which he thinks may, with the appropriate manipulation and co-ordination of measurements and theoretical constructions, lead to light being shed upon the problem. Ideas as to the appropriate manner of control must *precede* the experimentation and research. The appropriate 'facts' will yield their secrets only when wooed in the right way.

2. It is assumed that the world, the cosmos is orderly. The term 'universe' suggests this orderliness. Thus 'laws', 'systems', and on the basis of these, predictions are possible which can be relied upon and put to the test. A problem occurs when the order expected does not appear in any given instances; when the law does not

co-ordinate the data as it was expected to, perhaps where it had done so in the past; when an instrument designed to make possible the acquisition of hoped for information hitherto not available, provides the researcher with unexpected and surprising data.

The expectation of a certain regularity is *assumed* by the researcher. But it is something which he never proves. It is taken for granted.

What happens when the expected regularity does not in any given instance show itself? The scientist must then try to offer an explanation of the unexpected. He will do this on the basis of the assumptions he makes and the theory and evidence he already has.

A famous case in point is that of the discovery of Neptune. The planet Uranus, it was noticed, was not following the orbit it was expected to. How could its erratic motion, its 'perturbations', be explained? Assuming the truth of the theory of gravitation, even at such great distances from the sun, an attempt was made to deduce accurately the existence and position of an hypothetical planet which could cause the aberrations of Uranus. The position of this body was calculated. It was then a matter of locating it (if the explanations were correct) in the heavens at the place calculated. Leverrier who had made the computations sent the calculation to Berlin where J. G. Galle with the necessary equipment at his service found the planet Neptune, the night after he had read the letter sent to him by Leverrier (1846). He was able to do so because he had the appropriate instruments to enable him to make the required observational checks, whereas other people who were also well on to the problem were unable to do so.

This is a good point to consider the meaning of *law* in science. Since the word is used in another fundamental sense there must be no confusion of the two basic meanings. In ethics a law *prescribes* what ought to be done. In science a law *describes* what has been observed to happen, and thus can be used as the basis of prediction. The law in science comes after the event. We can easily see the difference by taking examples: 'Thou shalt not steal' tells us what you are to do, how to regulate your conduct. It makes a certain demand on you and you can either accept or reject that demand. If you accept the demand you may or may not follow it.

Fact and Proof

Such a law states a certain imperative, makes a certain demand. If you do not follow the demand you 'break' the law.

Not so with a scientific law, which is a general statement made on the basis of sufficient observed examples. For an example take Boyle's law. It states that for a fixed mass of gas at a given temperature, the product of the pressure and volume is constant. Put somewhat differently, the volume of a given mass of an enclosed gas varies inversely with the pressure of the gas if the temperature is kept constant. This law is a statement which summarizes the results of observing various instances of the behaviour of different gases kept at constant temperatures, and of measuring precisely the relationship between pressure and volume. On the strength of numerous instances the general statement is made. A law is a statement based upon a number of instances but extended from the limited number of instances which are considered sufficient to establish it to all possible instances. The general statement or law is thus made the basis for the prediction of further instances. One can thus 'demonstrate' the validity of Boyle's law by performing the simple experiments described in the school textbooks.

A scientific law is thus based upon a sufficient number of observed regularities from the past. The regularity thus observed is then projected into the future. The statement of the particular regularity observed is called a *law*. It is thus not right to speak (as some people used to do for example about miracles) about the breaking of the laws of nature. You cannot break a law of nature, let alone think that there's something wrong if you do. That is to confuse the scientific meaning of law with the ethical meaning of it. It should be clear that the scientific idea of law (which we shall take up again in the next chapter) has to do with probabilities and regularities. It is not a matter of 'proof'.

This is an important question for our discussion because people often demand proof before they will accept something, or at least make a show of doing so. The idea is that anything less than proof is not worthy of acceptance. It is even said sometimes, 'If it can't be demonstrated, I can't believe it.' When questions about religion arise, they are put into the category of the unproved and so set aside. Quite apart from the contradiction in the objection—You do not have to *believe* what is proved, you know its truth—it is simply claiming far too much to say that we only accept as

Religion and Science

true that which is proved. Most of what we accept as true is very far from proved. Indeed proof in peculiarly irrelevant in the most important matters of life.

We do not expect the trustworthiness of our friends to be proved before we shall call them our friends. A man cannot have the fidelity of his loved one proved to him. If he waited for that before he trusted her or married her, he would never trust and remain a batchelor for ever. In making a business deal one moves forward accepting the element of risk involved in the hope that one's discernment and acumen will be rewarded. There can be no question of any proof for any attitude which anticipates the future. We do take, as we ought to take, important decisions and initiate important actions on the strength often of quite a low degree of probability. We certainly do not often if ever demand proof before we decide or act. To make out we do is simply very far from the truth of real life.

Nor does the scientist 'prove'. He may provide evidence with a sufficient degree of probability to make his point. For him as for all of us, probability is the guide of life.

Since the idea is such an important one, we shall pursue it a little further and ask when it *is* appropriate to talk about proof? We say that something is probable, and not merely possible, when we have come to have an expectation of it. We also say that something is probable when we are not certain about it. We might even speak of it as being 'only probable'. Thus we set the concept between certainty on the one hand and possibility on the other. More than possible but less than proved. It's all a question of the nature of the evidence. The more compelling the evidence the greater the probability of the assertion or conclusion based upon it or drawn from it. Since evidence as we say 'impresses' or 'compels', we speak about degrees of certainty on the basis of probability.

But when do we talk about proof? about demonstration?

The obvious answer is in geometry. One remembers the letters Q. E. D. (*Quod erat demonstrandum* = what was to be proved (supply) has been proved). If you start off with certain things given, taken for granted (what the Greeks called first principles, *archai*) you can make certain *deductions* which lead you to a certain conclusion, which you can then say has been proved. Take the following example of a valid syllogism. A syllogism is a bit of reasoning

Fact and Proof

with one logical step in it. You start off with two propositions and conclude from these a third. So:

A. All men are fallible.   *B.* Some men are fallible
    Joe was a man.   Joe was a man.

What can be concluded from these pairs of propositions? Let us add a third:

C. Sue thinks all men are fallible.
    Sue thinks Joe is a man.

From *A* it should rightly be concluded that Joe is fallible, proved. From *B* it should be concluded that we do not know whether Joe is fallible. From *C* it should be concluded that Sue is thinking straight only if she concluded that Joe is fallible. If Sue concluded from *B* that Joe might be infallible, we could not, on the basis of the syllogism refute her. The difference between *A* and *B* is that *A*'s major premise, the first proposition, is universal (all includes every man), whereas in the second, *B*, it is not.

Take another example:

D. Some dogs are four-footed.
    Fido is a dog.

But now, let us begin to fill in more concretely what 'some' in the major premise means. Some means: *i*, 99 per cent; *ii*, 50 per cent; *iii*, 1 per cent. Taking these different meanings let us see what conclusions we may draw. If 99 per cent of dogs are four-footed, we would say that if Fido be a dog there is a very high degree of probability that he will be four-footed. In case *ii* we would speak of a 50/50 chance. In case *iii* we would say that the odds are steeply against his being four-footed. These things we can say purely in terms of the form of the propositions. We could even use nonsense words, for example:

E. All boojams are welk
    Perelo is a boojam
    Therefore Perelo is welk.

Since that is only odd, it is better to express the relationship of propositions in symbols, so

F. All *A* is *B*
    x is *A*
    Therefore *x* is *B*.

That amounts to proof. It is logical and formal, i.e. has to do with relations between propositions.

We said earlier that if we take the major premise as *given* we have a basis of argument. But how do we ever get into the position of being able to speak of *'all* men' or *all* anything else? There are such cases. But we would have to specify the cases to establish the 'first principle'. This is not done by logic but by examination of the evidence. In the following syllogism what is important is that the first principle, the major premise is *established*. It is here not simply a matter of definition.

G. All present at the meeting were informed of the bonus.
    Jean was present at the meeting.
    Jean was informed of the bonus.

It is established, in this case, in certain quite specifiable ways. People at the meeting were not asleep, nor were unduly disturbed while the announcement was being made. All were able to hear well since the public address system was working and the acoustics of the hall were good. People were listening. I heard what was said clearly at the back of the hall. That is enough to establish, with a high degree of probability, the major premise. Since Jean, in the minor premise, is included in the 'all' of the major premise, it follows of necessity that she was informed of the bonus, *if* it is true that she was present at the meeting. But that is an empirical statement, and is established therefore on the basis of evidence of the appropriate kind.

She greeted me as we were going into the hall, and I saw her coming out. (Of course I recognize her!) If I want confirmation of my conviction based on the premises of the argument, I can say to her, 'What did you think of that?' after the meeting. If she makes a specific reference to the bonus and does not simply say 'Jolly good!' her answer will confirm what I had already concluded on the basis of both the premises. Since these premises were based upon empirical evidence of a positive nature the conclusion I drew had a high degree of probability. Because it did I could be certain about drawing it.

Fact and Proof

So in science in a test case, an experiment, a series of tests may provide the basis for argumentation. If the conclusion is put out as a law it will mean that the 'all' expressed or implicit in the statement will be projected into the future. But since the 'all' is based upon past experience, and hedged about with qualifications, the conclusion will be probably rather than strictly proved. The degree of probability will in some cases be so high that, for all intents and purposes, the scientist will take it *as if* proved and say 'It is established that...' Where he is not so sure, he will present the propositions reporting his convictions as a *hypothesis* rather than a law. Further and more extensive experience may invalidate the proposition as it stands. The point here is that it is just not on to speak of the scientist as the only one who offers proof of what he says, while quite different procedures are found in other areas of human life and thought, and then to set up the scientist as *the* model of how knowledge is to be achieved, all other methods being inferior.

The establishing of the results of science takes place within a framework of theory, which theory guides in the gathering and assessment of the facts. Acceptance of theory is like the acceptance of rules of a game. You play the game taking them for granted and not questioning them when the game is proceeding smoothly. The scientist can do research successfully without his constantly referring to the rules of his game. But there were times in the history of science when the rules of the particular games being played were called into question. The reason for this was because scientists had difficulty in solving their problems according to the rules which they had assumed. Some problems could not be solved by the rules of the game given by Ptolemy, or by playing phlogiston games à la Priestley. Proof is 'proof' within the framework of a theory. When scientists disagree and keep on disagreeing on major issues the theory will undergo a change and new 'proofs' will be tried out.

Summary and Conclusion

We cannot entertain as an objection to religious perspective, that the attitudes of the believer and the modes of logic in which these are expressed, are so different from those of the scientist, that they are not respectable; nor, conversely, that the scientific attitude and logic requires an attitude of mind that is of necessity antagonistic

Religion and Science

to that of the believer. Specifically, it is just not true that there is a necessary conflict because the scientist simply deals with facts and proof, while the believer relies upon feelings and theory.

Discussion Questions

Try to state as concisely as possible what the distinction between Botany, Biology and Zoology is.

How can you be sure that 'All men are mortal' when you have not been in a position to examine the evidence for *all* cases?

How can you be sure that the following propositions are correct?

> Men are stronger and taller than women.
> Water boils at 100 degrees centigrade.
> Children under six cannot understand the meaning of determinism.
> Insurance companies make profits.
> Religious people believe in (some sort of) God.
> Religious rituals, stories and doctrines have meaning.
> Jane and I will probably make a lot of money and have a happy marriage.

Would you weigh these probabilities seriously? Why? For what purpose?

> It is probable that mother will have supper ready at eight o'clock.
> It is improbable that there is an electrician in the house.

Discuss how a judgement about probability might influence the way you act.

If the distinction between the religious and the scientific approach to reality is not that between belief and proof, what differences are there?

4 | The Scientist and His Facts

OBSERVATIONS constitute an important part of the scientist's procedure. But, we all observe. People have observed things for centuries. But you can observe and not see. If the mind is blank the observation is likely to be unseeing. Where the pencil-in-hand accompanies the problem-in-mind, observation will be to some purpose. Looking is one thing, seeing is another, and understanding is yet another. One looks more carefully and to some purpose if one has some idea before and while he looks where to look and what to look for. One can realize the significance of what one has observed if one gives it careful and critical consideration afterwards, trying to fit it into a pattern built up from what one has seen and understood before. Haphazard observation may yield few (if any) positive results of relevance for the building up of a careful science. People had seen apples falling to the ground for donkey's years, but no one had thought about 'falling' as Newton did. No one fitted the phenomenon of falling things into a pattern that included the movement of planets. It was when what was observed was interpreted as bearing upon and illuminating a problem that the observation was directed to some constructive purpose.

The process of observation can be both intended and controlled. What you need to observe so as to achieve understanding may not present itself readily and naturally. It may have to be achieved by setting up a test situation, where the factors which are of importance can be controlled. You may have to construct instruments to make the required observation possible and measurement accurate, and so obtain data which would otherwise escape attention. Of course, one cannot create eclipses to order as one can induce hunger or disease in a guinea-pig. The setting-up of a test situation pre-supposes that the researcher has some ideas *before* he gets the results, that he is able to get results, which may be different from

Religion and Science

those he expects to get, because he has both the idea of a problem and hunches as to how the problem might be solved, and what sort of data are relevant to the solution of the problem.

This does not mean that he can predict the results which will follow from the use of the instruments. The psychologist builds intricate mazes to test the reactions of rodents. He may find something about animal behaviour which he did not expect. The astronomer builds a gigantic radio telescope, and later he gets the surprise of the century—pulsars and quasars.

Theory can prevent constructive observation. There was a struggle which had to be fought out before modern science could come into its own. The disciples of Aristotle had to be refuted before the new science could become accepted. The symbol of the new theories and attitude was an instrument, the telescope.

The Aristotelian philosopher said: 'The cosmos of the divine Aristotle, with its mystical, music-making spheres and crystal domes and the gyrations of its heavenly bodies and the oblique angle of the sun's orbit and the secrets of the satellite tables and the rich catalogue of constellations in the southern hemisphere and the inspired construction of the celestial globe, is a conception of such symmetry and beauty that we should do well to hesitate before disturbing that harmony.'

Galileo said, 'How would it be if you ... were now to observe these impossible as well as unnecessary stars through this telescope?'

The Mathematician said, 'It would be much more helpful, Signor Galileo, if you would tell us the reasons which lead you to the assumption that in the highest spheres of the immutable Heavens stars can move freely through space.'

To this Galileo replied, 'The reasons?—When a glance at the stars themselves and my own observations will demonstrate the phenomenon. Sir, the disputation is becoming absurd.'[1]

The instrument is the product of theory and the means of testing theory, by providing (it is hoped) the requisite evidence to bear out the theory that led to its creation. To develop and use an instrument means that one expects a certain kind of answer to the problem. When what takes place is different from what was expected new

[1] Bertold Brecht, *The Life of Galileo*, Scene Four, London, Methuen, 1960, pp. 51, 52.

work will have to be done, new theory produced, new experiments performed. So with the discovery of X-rays, for example. The glowing screen had been observed by others before Roentgen, but they did not make the 'discovery'. The glow pointed to the X-ray only when it had been sufficiently 'explained' by the development of adequate theory.

Scientific discoveries do take place by accident sometimes. But it takes a scientist to recognize the accident. Such accidents must be noticed, otherwise their relevance and importance could not be communicated. Such 'accidents' do not happen to the non-observant. They are noticed where there is an interest in and an understanding of their significance. It happens in a laboratory that an interesting growth takes place and is noticed by scientists working on a particular problem. They see the significance of what they see and penicillin comes into being. That 'seeing the significance of' is what makes a scientific fact. If it had not been noticed and had been thrown away it would of course have been there but nothing would have been discovered, no new fact would have become known. Natural occurrences may come and go unnoticed.

But a natural occurrence is a different kind of 'fact' if it is noticed and interpreted. It is difficult to know what an unnoticed happening—the falling of the log in the primeval forest—should be called. We would hardly call it a 'fact'. Facts are significant. Their significance is related to the framework of theory within which they are seen. The judgement that a fact is not worth noticing is no exception to the principle.

The idea of the scientist as the remote, impersonal, passive observer of facts that press themselves upon him; the image of the scientist as a concept-less, unbiased and indifferent researcher who just has the right sort of ears that can hear the facts speak is an illusion. He must *make* the facts speak. It is the speaking that makes the 'fact' a fact, that is a noteworthy and significant datum illuminating a particular problem. The activity of the scientist is not just the gathering together of the 'facts'. At every stage of the game there is theory. The story of science is the story of what happens to its theories. Theory precedes and directs, modifies and is modified by, follows the discovery, the co-ordination and the assessment of the data.

This does not mean that any theory goes, that there is no control over the facts. Facts are objective. The sense in which they are objective is this. Anyone who is able to do the experiment, and interpret the data it attempts to co-ordinate can agree that the problem is amenable to the proposed solutions.

That is the kind of objectivity which we have been contending for in this chapter as opposed to the objectivity which demands facts and facts only. We have argued that there is no such kind of objectivity. That does not mean that there is no objectivity. We shall consider this question further in our next chapter.

The theory can be tested by appropriate means within the community of scientists. This does not mean that it will be. It means that it could be, should it be necessary.

So, while it is true that science as a progressive enterprise of a human community depends upon experimentation for its results and its status, the fact is that people who study science do not do the crucial experiments. They accept what they are told on the basis of the teacher's word or on the authority of the textbook, not because they have examined the evidence for themselves. Mind you, they assume that if it were necessary they could, or at least somebody would, repeat the experiment. They assume that the theory that lies behind the experiment is correct, as well as the unexamined underlying assumptions (orderliness of the world, amenability of the world to scientific approaches, etc.).

The scientist takes assertions about fact on authority, as does the non-scientist. You do not have to repeat the history of science to be a scientist.

To make the point about the importance of theory for science, we shall consider briefly the following terms: concepts, laws, theories.

The following are examples of *concepts* which have been and some of which are now employed in scientific work: phlogiston, ether, gravitation, neutron, wave-motion, energy, quantum, field.

What is 'observed' is related by means of the use of concepts. The scientist has to think about what he sees, before, while and after he sees it. Sometimes he cannot 'see' but by means of instruments and machines may be able to get a report. He has carefully considered what sort of instrument is suitable for the particular piece of work he is to undertake. When the data are being collected,

The Scientist and His Facts

they are also being interpreted. What is observed is expressed in a theoretical framework. In this way it receives significance. It is explained by being put within such a framework along with other data.

So, for example, energy (one of the examples given above) is not directly observed. It is not a 'brute fact' waiting for someone to find it as an objective datum in the scheme of things. It is a mental construction which, like many other such theoretical ideas, enables the scientist to co-ordinate and so up to a point to understand, what he experiences. Meaningful experience thus consists of observed data plus interpreting concepts.

A scientific *law* is as we have seen a statement describing observed regularities. Its application is based upon the assumption that what has been a regularly observable feature of nature will continue to be such. On the basis of this assumed regularity, predictions—an essential part of scientific activity—are made as to what is to be expected in the future.

Pause a moment and consider that there is nothing to prove the regularity. It is taken for granted. We may say that because something has happened a certain way ninety-nine times we can expect it to happen the same way the hundredth time. But it may not. The probability may be high that a certain event or series of events or kind of event may take place. But scientists are not unhappy when their predictions do not come true. Falsification of expectations may be as important as verification. Indeed it is possible to define the scientific as that which is capable of falsification. The point here is that expectation on the basis of probability is based on an *assumption* or upon a series of assumptions. Regularity is a basic concept assumed without proof in order to get the scientific enterprise going.

A *theory* is a general statement further removed still from direct observation or 'experience' than a law or a concept. It is capable of co-ordinating a whole range of laws and observable data. Its function is to suggest possible relationships of a kind which can be put to the test, thus making possible further exploration into the possibility of co-ordinating data. It is in the formation of useful theories that the imaginative genius of the scientist is to be seen. He knows the 'state of the subject': what data are available, how they have been co-ordinated in existing theories, and the usefulness and limitations of previous theories, which hypotheses have fallen by the way, and so on. The creative scientist takes it all in, but does more. He suggests a better alternative explanation, which can as adequately or more adequately co-ordinate the same data. A better explanation can either more adequately co-ordinate the same data, or include within its compass a wider range of data. A theory which encompasses more data is obviously, other things being equal, more adequate than one which encompasses less.

There have been conflicts between religion and science not only because the criticism has been made from the side of science that the religious are not really dealing with facts, but also because from the side of religion there has been a misunderstanding of the *function* of scientific theory. A scientific theory attempts the co-ordination and interpretation on the large scale of almost limitless data, e.g. the theory of evolution, or of relativity. The scientist is not so committed to existing structures of theory that he would never change. Revolutions of scientific thinking do take place. If the religious believer feels threatened by the implications of scientific theory and thinks that the right approach to be taken is to attack the theory, then he is quite at liberty to do so. If he makes his case, it will be because he will be able to provide a better theory, which will perform the same function as that one which he is attacking. What is not for him in dispute is the function of scientific theory.

It should be clear, even after such a preliminary statement as this, that the idea of the scientist as dealing with 'facts and facts only' is a myth. His imaginative powers are in play when creative work is done. In this respect he is no different from the poet, the prophet, the theologian or the historian.

Summary and Conclusion

The objection cannot be sustained that the scientific attitude is either so unique as to produce unique certainty, or is to be taken as normative for all modes of inquiry, on the basis of its concern for facts. The question of its uniqueness and normativeness must be discussed particularly in each particular case. At all stages of science there is theoretical construction, which is revised when it becomes necessary.

The Scientist and His Facts

Discussion Questions

What is a Scientific Problem?

How do problems arise in Science?

Read the following passage, then tackle the questions which follow:

When Galileo caused balls, the weights of which he had himself previously determined, to roll down an inclined plane; when Toricelli made the air carry a weight which he had calculated beforehand to be equal to that of a definite column of water; or in more recent times, when Stahl changed metals into oxides, and oxides back into metal, by withdrawing something and then restoring it, a light broke upon all students of nature. They learned that reason has insight only into that which it produces after a plan of its own, and that it must not allow itself to be kept, as it were, in nature's leading strings, but must itself show the way with principles of judgement based upon fixed laws, constraining nature to give answer to questions of reason's own determining. Accidental observations, made in obedience to no previously thought-out plan, can never be made to yield a necessary law, which alone reason is concerned to discover. Reason, holding in one hand its principles, according to which alone concordant appearances can be admitted as equivalent to laws, and in the other hand the experiment which it has devised in comformity with these principles, must approach nature in order to be taught by it. It must not, however, do so in the character of a pupil, who listens to everything that the teacher chooses to say, but of an appointed judge, who compels the witnesses to answer questions which he himself has formulated. Even physics, therefore, owes the beneficent revolution in its point of view entirely to the happy thought, that while reason must seek in nature, not fictitiously ascribe to it, whatever as not being knowable through reason's own resources has to be learnt, if learnt at all, only from nature, it must adopt as its guide, in so seeking, that which it has put into nature. It is thus that the study of nature has entered on the secure path of science, after having for so many centuries been nothing but a process of merely random groping.
Immanuel Kant, preface to the *Critique of Pure Reason*, B. xiii–xiv.

State the view of the relation between theory and experiment of the above passage.

Religion and Science

Find examples of discoveries made in science at the time of the writing of the *Critique*, which illustrate the point being made.

Does accident play a part in the progress of science? Is a 'scientific accident' an exception to the principle expounded by Kant? Collect some modern examples and discuss them with it in mind.

5 | Subject and Object

'FACTS are facts' is a familiar saying. One that is most easy to misunderstand. It suggests the idea that facts are obtrusive things that leap out at you, and you cannot help but say, 'Yes, yes, of course!' There's no interference from the mind of the subject who has the facts jump at him. Facts are objective, real, true, 'there' 'out there'.

The word 'subjective' is sometimes used of ideas that are held only by the individual, so that it comes to mean idiosyncratic, perhaps even eccentric. If an opinion is dubbed 'subjective' the intention is conveyed that it is not worth too much attention, that it is one person's idea and he may not be very reliable. A 'subjective' interpretation means one that has not received the acknowledgement of those who know.

But be careful. Let us distinguish between subjective and what we shall call 'subjectivistic'. Every observation, every judgement I make is subjective in the sense that it is I, a subject, who is making it. But the judgement I make may be the right judgement, amenable to some kind of public test and judged by many people to be as I make it. Or it may not. For we do have ways of putting claims to the test which we all in some measure recognize, for example: taking account of all that should be taken account of; relying upon the right sources of information; not prejudging the case before all due consideration has been taken.

We make the right judgements when we deal with the evidence rightly. Facts are established on evidence. Evidence is evaluated according to particular ideas. We consider, for example, whether what is said to have happened comes within the range of what we would think possible. We consider the various bits of the evidence and try to piece them together. We consider what this bit of evidence means, and what that. Then what both of them mean when they are put together. So there is a most important part which interpretation plays in both getting a complete picture of something, say of an accident, and then in coming to a judgement about it.

What then about the saying 'facts are facts'? It is a truism that what you see depends on how you look. Perspectives make a difference. People do disagree about the facts. They argue about what the facts are, as well as arguing what they mean. In some cases, we cannot get away from the factuality, nor can we avoid disagreement as to the meaning of the facts. How then do we go about assessing the judgement which we or someone else has made about the facts?

'The principal difficulty in your case,' remarked Holmes, in his didactic fashion, 'lay in the fact of there being too much evidence. What was vital was overlaid and hidden by what was irrelevant. Of all the facts which were presented to us, we had to pick just those which we deemed to be essential, and then piece them together in their order, so as to reconstruct this very remarkable chain of events. I had already begun to suspect Joseph.... When I heard that someone had been so anxious to get into the bedroom, in which no one but Joseph could have concealed anything... my suspicions all changed to certainties, especially as the attempt was made on the first night upon which the nurse was absent, showing that the intruder was well acquainted with the ways of the house.'[1]

In the case of the Naval Treaty we have an interesting statement of the way in which discovery of the 'truth' is arrived at. First, there is the weighing of the evidence from among the many facts. Not every fact is a piece of evidence. A process of sorting out has to be done. Evidence is fact which bears upon a certain question. So, second, an idea as to what the truth is, a hunch, a hypothesis, a suspicion is worked out, and then it is brought back to the facts. It's a two-way traffic. The hunch is based upon the facts, and then is tested by the facts. The facts are interpreted by the hunch, and then shown to be relevant or not. Obviously we do not call the interpretative process by which the detective moves from suspicion to hypothesis to probability to proof (the confession of the criminal) a subjective one, even if in the hands of a master it is so highly

[1] Arthur Conan Doyle, *The Memoirs of Sherlock Holmes*, London, Penguin, 1955, p. 233.

individualistic. Since we may be *persuaded* of the correctness of a particular interpretation by appeal to evidence, we must be careful not to make hasty judgements when we have not considered as much evidence as has the subject making the judgement and presenting it for our consideration. It's not that the facts are unavailable to us as they were to him. It's that we have not seen what he sees as significant for the making of a proper judgement. We may not have had the discernment to make the judgement. But, if we were given some guidance we might be better off. When once the judgement has been pointed out to us, we can agree that that is the way it ought to have been made, and that we would have made it had we been really discerning. By this we mean, had we looked at the crucial facts, those which provided a clue to the whole. Some of us are not very good at discerning a reasonable pattern in certain constellations of facts. We have to depend for that on other people.

We have said that people do argue about the facts. It is a favourite device in detective stories to have the junior, or the police, or maybe the rival detective make out a most convincing case for the particular theory he has devised, only to have it completely shattered by the master mind of the brilliant investigator, as in the following:

Major Riddle said decisively:
'If it's murder, it's up to you to prove it. If you ask me, I say it's definitely suicide. Did you notice what the girl said about a former agent having swindled old Gervase? I bet Lake told that tale for his own purposes. He was probably helping himself a bit, Sir Gervase suspected it and sent for you because he didn't know how far things had gone between Lake and Ruth. Then this afternoon Lake told him they were married. That broke Gervase up! It was 'too late' now for anything to be done. He determined to get out of it all. In fact his brain, never very well balanced at the best of times, gave way. In my opinion that's what happened. What have you got to say against it?'

Poirot stood still in the middle of the room.

'What have I to say? This: I have nothing to say against your theory—but it does not go far enough. There are certain things it does not take into account.'

'Such as?'

'The discrepancies in Sir Gervase's moods today, the finding of

Religion and Science

Colonel Bury's pencil, the evidence of Miss Lingard as to the order in which people came down to dinner, the position of Sir Gervase's chair when he was found, the paper bag which had held oranges, and finally, the all-important clue of the broken mirror.'

Major Riddle stared.

'Are you going to tell me that that rigmarole makes *sense*?' he asked.

Hercule Poirot replied softly:

'I hope to make it do so—by tomorrow.'[2]

It's amusing because once it's pointed out the correct solution is so obvious. And it is true that sometimes the simplest solution is the best. Not always. If it's truth we are after, we must sometimes not be led to ask for simplicity. The degree of simplicity will depend upon the complexity of the problem with which we are concerned. It will sometimes be a most complex matter to devise the sort of tests which we need. In some cases we shall simply not have the evidence we need, or would desire. There are occasions where two theories are proposed to account for the same set of facts. For example the Nobel prize was given to Arrhenius for his theory of dissociation. Later Debye received the same prize for criticizing it.

Arrhenius put forward his 'ionic theory' in 1887 to account for the behaviour of charged particles in an electrolyte (a solution which conducts electricity and which is changed in the process). The theory proposed was quite satisfactory—as far as it went. It was true for weak electrolytes but not for the more common strong electrolytes. Further observations led to Debye's theory, which was able to account for more of the data than was Arrhenius's and so proved itself to be of greater explanatory worth. He was able to apply it to both weak and strong electrolytes, whereas Arrhenius dissociation theory was applicable only to weak electrolytes.

Light has been explained as both wave and particle. Such theories appeal to facts, but are not subjectivistic—they are appropriate to data which have come within the range of experience, even if they seem to conflict.

This leads us to a most important point. To be impartial does not mean that one does not have explanatory hypotheses or theories.

[2] Agatha Christie, 'Dead Man's Mirror', is *My Best Mystery Story*, London, Faber & Faber, 1965, pp. 81–2.

There is no such thing as such impartiality. One can take account of the perspective from which one sees things. To be impartial means that one sees one's own perspective as part of the total reality, and recognizes the fact of alternative explanations. Let us suggest three tests, then, which will keep us from extremes, extreme positivism (only the facts) and extreme subjectivism (only the opinions of the subject):

1. Taking into account of conditioning factors involved in coming to the particular conclusions.

It does and should make a difference to the way we evaluate a person's statements that we know something of the positions he takes. Particularly, but not only, in the social sciences, it is the perspective that makes the writer's work both valuable, interesting and it may be sometimes, dangerous. For example, let us suppose we are interested in racial relations. There is a certain detachment which is required for a scientific account and the reliable theoretical account will be impartial if it maintains such detachment. The understanding represented in the scientific account, say of racial hatred, can be employed to reduce or to foster racial prejudice. The knowledgeable person is in an advantageous position whatever his intentions are. What will he do with his knowledge of the facts? How will he 'use' them? That is an important question. To be aware of the perspective of the particular writer enables one to make a balanced judgement about what he says. One cannot always take all the scientist says for science.

That the perspective must most seriously be taken into account in evaluating the scientist's position is not only true of the work of the scholar. It is true on other levels. Our own opinions are influenced by our background, even to the things we seldom think about. That we seldom think about some things is also due to conditioning factors. It is most easy to overlook such things. But if we are going to be fair to ourselves we can't.

2. Inter-subjective testability.

This phrase implies that we can standardize personal evaluations by means of agreed-upon conventions, rules or norms. If the doting father makes the judgement, 'My son is running fast', and then learns that the school record was twice as fast as the boy is now running, then he will have to revise his judgement against this timed and witnessed standard. The experience in an agreed-upon form

Religion and Science

acts as a norm for future judgements. Standard forms of measurement have been accepted: metres, minutes, seconds. The performance has also been witnessed and recorded.

If we put our right hand in a bowl of cold water, our left hand in a bowl of hot water and then put both hands into a bowl of lukewarm water, we are likely to get different sensations in the two hands. The right hand will feel warm and the left hand will feel cold. But the water cannot be hot and cold at the same time. But the term 'hot' and 'cold' can be given a meaning that could be generally agreed upon. If the water in the third bowl were, let us say, twenty degrees centigrade, we would agree, however our hand felt when it was put into the bowl, that the water in it was lukewarm. The measurement provides a check upon our judgement about the water there. If we feel lukewarm water as cold, and someone else feels it as hot, we shall explain the difference by speaking about the conditioning factors that preceded the making of the judgement. But we could point out the thermometer reading as a standard that could be agreed upon. Under certain circumstances we also have to remember that the measuring, the putting to the test, may alter the total situation, and allow for that too. You can measure the velocity of an electron or its position but not both at the same time.

If a father and a mother disagree about the advisability of a certain suitor for their daughter's hand, it may be possible to agree on some sort of a yardstick, some thinkers even saying that the considerations can be measured in quantitative terms. If happiness is the standard and we can measure the amount of happiness likely to result and set it against the probable unhappiness, we might be able to work out a sum and on the basis of that sum judge the course of action which seemed likely to produce the greater happiness and propose that that was good. So if father and mother disagreed it might be because they thought differently about what constituted happiness. 'Well, he's rich and will be able to give her a very, very comfortable life.' 'Yes, but she's an outdoor girl, and she's never been happy in the city, where he has his life.'

So one can put up arguments on both sides of the case as one can in other cases, say, for example with reference to abortion or euthanasia.

If it's a question about good and bad, and one person says:

Subject and Object

'That is good', while another says 'That is bad', since there is a patent contradiction, one has to make qualifications. Either, 'Well, that's because they are looking at it from different perspectives!' when you are sympathetic to both, or 'Well! Of course, what do you expect, when he's had such a background!' if you disagree.

So one could say, 'Well! You don't expect the father to think differently do you, when he's always had it drummed into him that the most important thing in life is making money and getting things.' Or, in another case, 'Well, she's been taught that life is to be saved at any cost and that there are no exceptions to that principle.'

3. Exposure to the opinions to be found within the knowledgeable community appropriate to the particular kind of question involved.

The third test should be precisely understood. There is such a formidable thing as 'expert opinion' about the matters the experts are experts about. It frightens the layman, who sometimes finds himself with the distressing sense of being outdistanced. The strange thing is that in matters of religion, people often feel that their opinions are worthy of the same consideration as those of professional theologians. Why should they? While by no means endorsing the idea that the majority in any given sphere are always right, we must consider that body of opinion, fact and method which have been developed in any given discipline before making hasty judgements. It provides a check against the subjectivity of the individual. This means that a point of view may have to be made convincing before it is accepted. That is all to the good.

Summary and Conclusion

Facts are *established* by processes which can be specified, in relation to evidence which has to be established as evidence according to rules and theories. Since facts are presented and assessed in a particular light, through particular perspectives, a consideration of the process of interpretation involved in making factual propositions is demanded. We should overcome the naïveté sometimes found in highly sophisticated people of closing the argument by appeal to 'facts' which need no further discussion.

Religion and Science

Discussion Questions

Are there opinions you would alter if you found people disagreed with you? Are there some that you would stick to under any circumstances?

Ask why you have answered the way you have.

What is the difference between

> seeing an accident and then giving testimony,
>
> observing the goings on in a researcher's laboratory and giving an account of them afterwards,
>
> believing in a person and giving an account of your trust.

Why do historians disagree about the 'facts'?

6 | *What is Possible?*

A YOUNG boy was abandoned by his parents while an infant. He was brought up in the woods by gazelles. When he was finally discovered he was sixteen years old. He met human beings for the first time. He could not speak, but only emit grunts. He had to be taught to eat and drink in human ways, since he would lie flat on his belly to lap up the water. He could run at sixty miles an hour.

A mother realizing that her child was trapped under a car, went to the vehicle and exerting all the strength she had was able to lift the back of the car so that the child could be freed.

These examples were both taken from the newspapers.

You can't believe everything you read in the newspaper. Or elsewhere for that matter. So you have to use your judgement. We can learn something rather important from the way in which we come to a judgement about whether we consider what we have read to be possible, if we will give attention. What factors make us decide one way or the other?

Could he really run at sixty miles an hour? How would we decide? Something like this, I think. The world's best athletes can run a mile in four minutes. That is going at fifteen miles an hour for four minutes. They are exhausted at the end of it. To run at sixty miles an hour would mean going 1,760 yards a minute, which is about thirty yards a second (29.33 to be exact!). Even a gazelle boy has only two legs. Could he really make them cover twenty-nine yards a second, and keep that up? I doubt it! The newspaper report must be incorrect on this detail. What did we do? We mustered from the range of our experience relevant facts and applied them to the issue under question. These facts were about athletes, about the capacity of human legs and muscles, and about newspaper reporters (they sometimes make mistakes). This set of considerations drawn from our experience weighed negatively in reference to the matter in question.

Could she really lift the car up? 'Car' may mean a small mini, we tell ourselves. In times of great emergency or fear a surge of adrenalin in the blood stream can give extraordinary strength. This would certainly be a case of extreme anguish for the mother. Yes, it is possible. We have, in this case, drawn upon our experience again, and put together from it certain elements which led us to consider first that the act was possible, and later that it was probable.

Please notice, and we mention it only in passing now, that to consider something possible (or not possible) is one sort of judgement. It is not identical with saying that something did (or did not) happen. We have to look at the evidence as well. For what could happen might not in fact happen. All kinds of things that could happen do not happen. What is within the range of possibility, even of expectation, may not come to be actual, e.g. my climbing the Matterhorn, my students passing their examinations, the city fathers exercising restraint, the lamp-post being painted yellow. Whether or not what is possible takes (or took) place is established by accepting the evidence for its occurrence, as being sufficient. To produce conviction that evidence must impress itself upon us as satisfactory. We have to rest the case at some point.

Now let us suppose we had an account of a boy who ran at 18 m.p.h. We would be likely to believe it. Say 20 m.p.h. What then? Say 22? 25? 30? While we would be ready to agree that it was possible for a boy to run at 18 m.p.h. we would (I suppose) deny the possibility of his running at 30 m.p.h. Tell me, if you can, where between the two credibility would be so strained that you would begin to make a negative judgement? We have a pretty good idea concerning what is possible and what is not, even if we find it difficult to specify the limits between them.

In the woman-car-child case, we would make some reservations. 'You'll understand that the word "car" can stand for different kinds and weights of vehicle. I'm not saying that she could lift up any kind of car. I'm saying that given this latitude in the use of the term "car" there would be some kinds of vehicle she could lift up, so we'll let the report stand. But now if it came to a corporation bus, *that* would be a different matter.' Indeed it would. That would

What is Possible?

be to cross the gap of credibility. Women, men, not even weight-lifters raise the backs of corporation buses. It just is not done, So, judging from our experience, that would be just a tall story.

In each case reflection on our experience has provided a certain pre-disposition to the report in view. There are occasions when it is necessary to suspend judgement, or to keep an open mind. 'Well, it looks pretty unlikely you know, but something may turn up and clarify the whole business. Who knows?' But you can't keep an open mind on everything, and you've got to act on your experience. Sometimes the reasonable course to take is the following: to say that in view of my experience and the evidence to hand, I hold that it is not possible but, having said that, to be ready to consider new evidence if and when it becomes available. Prejudice is that state of mind which refuses to take the appropriate step upon due consideration. It might be prejudiced to affirm, to deny or to suspend judgement in any particular case. It would depend on the case.

Can we evolve a decisive norm or rule for the admission and refusal of what purports to be evidence? How can we say what counts as evidence? How can we say that something is established? If we are going to be open-minded we must entertain what might possibly count as evidence and examine it with certain rules in mind. On the other hand it is prejudice not to close the mind when it should be closed. If justified, we must say, 'It can't have happened. So I can't entertain evidence that it did.' A certain open-mindedness is prejudicial. We should not entertain what should not be entertained. But we have to make an initial decision as to what we will let count as evidence.

There is one barrier which we ourselves cannot cross, and that is the barrier marked out by our own experience, by 'human' experience. Here the big problem is that while we know what we personally have experienced, we rely upon *report* for what other people have experienced. When it comes to the past we rely on reports that have been handed down to us, and if we are going to be intelligent we must be critical about such reports.

An example will help to make this clear.

We would not accept reports that witches had been observed flying. We would not believe someone who said that he had seen witches. We are not children any more. We would go a step further and say that people who believed such reports should not have believed them. They were responsible for their gullibility and credulity. We say this because we think that people should not be carried away by a kind of social hysteria and have failed to examine the evidence. In the case of believing and judging stories of witches, it led to horrible results. We feel that such results were so tragically possible because people were so foolishly superstitious. We judge them foolish and responsible, because they let themselves be carried away. The reason for our response is that we do not find such purported events taking place within our own experience, nor do we get credible reports, or reports of any kind witnessing to the occurrence of such events by our contemporaries.

For we rely upon reports of what other people experience for our knowledge of the *present*. Our judgement concerning what is possible is based upon reports which we take to be credible. What we consider to be possible is thus based on our first hand evidence (our own experience), second hand evidence (reports of the experience of other human beings) and upon our personal assessment of such evidence.

Our critical judgement concerning what is possible is based upon our present experience. But our present experience is limited in many ways. We cannot really maintain when speaking about *present experience* as a standard of judgement that we personally have had or are now having experiences which bear out *all* of our claims. We put together the evidence drawn from our own experience and from reported experiences of others which we consider feasible, since to deny them would bring strong witnesses against us. When we make our judgement in such a case we depend on the witness of a third party rather than personal experience of that to which the witness bears witness. Judgement about the truthfulness of reports and the truthworthiness of witnesses produces our understanding of what is and what is not possible. In this way we derive a standard for judging reports which we hear, for assessing the purported evidence which comes to our attention.

In a law court, the assumption is made that the people concerned in the making of decisions and judgements have some *common* experience and certain shared standards of judgement. If the jury must decide whether it was possible for the accused to do something he claimed to have done or concerning evidence that something has taken place, it is assumed that they would be able to communicate, discuss, make a judgement and come to some agreement on the basis of their 'present experience'. They may never have had to make such a decision before. But this does not mean that they cannot make that kind of judgement now. Whether they can or not will depend upon whether they are able to find some analogy, within the range of what they have accepted as present experience, to the act or event they are being called to consider as possible or impossible.

Summary and Conclusion

When assessing whether we shall believe something to be possible we are careful to define the terms of the proposition being considered. Then we refer to our own and to other people's experience. If what the report claims has some analogy within that experience we are likely to accept it as true. Otherwise we are not.

Discussion Questions

Find examples in newspapers or magazines of stories you

  (a) believe
  (b) do not know whether to believe or not
  (c) do not believe.

Account for why your attitudes are different in these different cases. What would you need to convince you that you should believe something you do not now believe? Is your criterion reasonable? Why should it be?

What is evidence? Who says so?

7 | *Miracles*

THERE are three kinds of question which have been asked about miracles.
1. Can miracles happen?
2. Did miracles happen?
3. What do the miracle stories reveal?

But first we had better try to get a minimum working definition of miracle. It is an unusual event in nature, in which persons are involved.

How does one answer these first two questions? If miracles have happened then they can happen. If something actually takes place there is then no question that it is possible. Evidence that something did take place, it would seem, is sufficient to show that it is possible. If it is quite certain that some kinds of unusual events just could not happen, then no evidence for them would count. We seem to be up against a dilemma. Do we have to come to some conclusion on question 1 before looking at question 2? Or, do we have to settle question 2 in order to answer question 1?

Before we take some examples consider question 3. In some instances we can shelve the preceding questions (1 and 2) by trying to get a meaning out of the miracle story. 'Even if', we might say, 'what the story says did not take place as it says, it has some meaning. Moreover it's a good story and well worth the telling.'

The real problem arises when the miracle story seems to ask us to accept what has not come within the range of our present experience *and* when the story seems well attested as historical evidence.

We shall take some examples.

From Zoroastrianism, the Parsee religion, comes the story of Vishtaspa's horse. It is found in a book written about A.D. 1200.

Miracles

Zoroaster had been put into prison as the result of a successful plot by his enemies, nobles and priests. This accomplished, the horse of Vishtaspa the king fell prone and could not budge, its four legs drawn up to its belly. Zoroaster sent a message from his prison cell to the king saying that he could cure the beast and was willing to do so, if certain conditions were met, namely that for each leg cured, the king would grant him a favour. The king sent for Zoroaster, and when he had granted the first favour, that he accept the faith, the right front leg was straightened. The other legs of the charger were healed as Vishtaspa granted Zoroaster's other boons: that Isfendir, the king's son, should fight for the faith; that the queen should embrace the religion; that the plotters against Zoroaster be brought to light and punished. This done, the noble beast leapt to his feet. Zoroaster had established himself, routed his enemies and made new converts.

This story is about a Zoroaster who has come to be revered as the founder of a great religion. He, like other great religious leaders and founders, had to undergo struggles and pain before his religion became established. A remarkable religion is remarkable in its coming into being. The very fact that it has come to be is occasion for wonder and for thankfulness on the part of its adherents. These preceding two sentences say in a straightforward manner what the story says in a figurative way. Whether the story is historically true in making this point is neither here nor there. Its point is made in either case. Given the right conditions an attitude of wonder and thankfulness is expressed and evoked in the telling of the myth. For that purpose it does not matter whether the story is factual. The question of its factuality is either never raised or is simply answered affirmatively. In the former case the belief is implicit. In the latter it is explicit. In both cases it would be uncritical.

Now this miracle story mentions the proper noun Vishtaspa. One tradition says that Zoroaster lived in the sixth and fifth centuries B.C. and an alternative one places him several centuries earlier. The name Vishtaspa (= Hystaspes, father of Darius the Mede) locates Zoroaster tradition at the later point in history and so acts as an historical confirmation of that date as the time of Zoroaster. But, needless to say, that sort of confirmation is (in this case) independent of the assessment of the function of the story itself. Similarly some of the miracle stories of Luke show Jesus as concerned for non-Jewish people. That point is made independent of the factuality of the details of the stories.

In later Buddhism many legends arose about the Buddha, Gotama Siddharta. He had by this time become an object of reverence and worship for many of his followers. The wonder that gives rise to such reverence and worship is directed towards the decisive events of the founder's life and out of it there emerges the story of a miraculous birth. It is a confession that in the case of Gotama, things that do not normally happen have happened. Religions of such a profundity and appeal as Buddhism do not simply happen. They are not ordinary events. The sense of wonder and thankfulness that Buddhism did arise and is a going concern is expressed in the legendary accretions which have embellished the birth story. Myth is here the language of devotion. A myth-creating devotion is a living devotion.

This is the story of the Buddha's birth.

Mahayama, the wife of King Suddhodana of Kapilavastu, dreamt one night of a white elephant entering her womb. She became pregnant and her womb became transparent like a crystal casket. She felt an urge to withdraw for meditation to the forest and there, while beneath a sal tree, she gave birth—from her side. The child was born in full awareness and looking like the young sun; he leapt on to the ground, and where he touched it there sprang up a lotus. He looked to the four cardinal points, to the four half points, above and below, and saw deities and men acknowledging his superiority. He made seven steps northward, a lotus appearing at each footfall. His birth was greeted by Asita, a sage from the Himalayas, who likened him to Skanda, son of Agni. Astrologers made the prediction that he would be a great emperor or he would renounce life and become a Buddha. He was named Siddharta at a great ceremony attended by eighty thousand relatives and one hundred and eight Brahmins, and was given a hundred godmothers. Mahayama, filled with joy, died two days after his birth. Her sister Prajapati, another of Suddhodana's wives, took charge of the infant.[1]

Miracles are associated with the great world religions. Of course religious people are not so naïve as to think that everything that is unusual, and that is told in the form of a miracle story in connection

[1] Veronica Ions, *Indian Mythology*, London, Paul Hamlyn, 1968, p. 128.

Miracles

with that religion, actually took place. Stories are told for different reasons: one very important reason for the creation of stories of a certain kind—myths—is to illustrate and communicate religious truth in a way that evokes thought and demands response, quite apart from the fact that it is easily remembered. The details of such myths do not have to be taken as accounts of literal events. So it must be quite clear that belief in miracle on the part of the believer is not necessarily uncritical. He will not swallow every story as historical fact, even if he considers it to be of great importance. Truth comes in many different forms. We must not think that the believer cannot tell the difference between one kind of story and another.

The claims involving miracle made by different religions can be stated in a minimum way, and also in a maximum way. A looker-on, assuming he could understand, might not allow the maximum which the believer would claim. But if he tried to understand he might be quite able to allow the miracle claim, at its minimum, so to speak.

We shall take some examples. With each of the religious figures we shall mention are ssociated unusual events and unusual claims.

Judaism makes the claim that there was an Exodus; that the Old Testament account which associates great wonders with Moses the leader of the slave people at the time of the Exodus is a true account; that the central act of the community, the Passover, is a memorial of the Exodus.

Islam traces its origin from unusual experiences that happened to Mohammed: that he received visions in the desert and was commanded to recite what he had seen and to make it known; that his attitude to these visions until persuaded otherwise, was negative; that when he began to lay claim to the visions and to recount them a new religion began.

Christianity points to the following data: there is a community that remembers the resurrection of Jesus Christ; the resurrection was that event which made possible the faith and the activity of that believing community; the New Testament gives the account of the beginnings of this community.

In each case there is pointing to a unique event. In each case a believing community traces its origin to these decisive events. Such would be the minimal statement about the event. As such the statement is clearly historical, and quite easy to verify, namely, by looking for the continuing existence of the particular community. If this fact (a certain community which believes certain things about its origin) is taken seriously we must then go one further step in the investigation. Since the believing community is making a truth claim, and also stressing that it is important to believe truth, the implications of the claim must be available for consideration. We are bound then to raise the historical question, the question about beginnings.

In the case of the Christian faith there are two sorts of question about its beginnings. 'How did Christianity begin?' is answered by referring to the course of events which can be reconstructed from the Gospels and from the Acts, namely the fear and the disappointment after the death of Jesus, the reports that Jesus had manifested himself, the waiting, the preaching and the response the Jerusalem crowd made to it. But the 'how' in the question may probe deeper. How did it come about that when the death of their leader had taken place the disciples did not scatter and come to nothing? Is this something which lies beyond our reach?

There are certain events which lie, so to speak, on two sides of the resurrection. On the one side there is the death and burial of Jesus, and on the other there is the faith of the early Christian community that Jesus rose. What is the reality that lies between these events? It seems to 'defy definition but demand explanation'. A miracle?

What happened after the death of Jesus to make possible the emergence of a believing community? What evidence is there for this event called 'resurrection'? Is there anything to the claim that is made by the Christian believer that the resurrection is a *revelation* of the purpose and the being of God?

Since the New Testament of Jesus Christ includes among other writings four interpretations of the man Jesus, and since in each of these there are miracles of various kinds associated with his activity, we shall find that we cannot take the Christian faith seriously unless we take the questions of miracles seriously.

The first two kinds of question about miracle: Are they possible? Did they happen? are answered positively from within the context of Christian faith. Since the community is a going concern, an understanding of it will involve that one ask the question about

Miracles

the happening at its origin. Part of the evidence bearing on this problem is the answer given from within the community to the third type of question: What do the miracles stories reveal? Indeed since the historical question, 'Did they happen?' is answered by the believer in the affirmative he then adds this other question, 'What do the miracles reveal?' Their significance is rooted in event. For revelation, the bringing about of new knowledge,[2] is claimed in connection with the initial miracle(s). Thus an open mind is required on the question of possibility and on the historical question if understanding is to result: one way or the other.

We might end up with a conflict. We are, let us say, not inclined to admit the possibility of miracle. But upon examining the evidence we might find that it is difficult to dispense with miracle and make sense of both the documentary evidence and the fact of continuing faith in the Christian community. Let us risk a quotation:

> Basically this is an historical question, and can only be answered by the canons of historical criticism. What we must do is to lay aside, as far as possible, all preconceived notions about the possibility or impossibility of miracles and study the traditions recorded in the gospels to see how far back we can trace them—whether we can take them back to Jesus himself. Above all, we must remember that the cast-iron law of cause and effect, while an indispensable working hypothesis for the scientist, is no more than a hypothesis, and in this connection the scientist ought not to be allowed to dictate to the historian in advance of what the results of his investigation should be. If we find the results of historical criticism conflict with the modern scientific world-view we ought in principle to be ready to widen our world view to make room for those results.[3]

The first possibility is that our assessment of what is possible is called into question one way or the other. The second is that what has been called revelation may become clear to us. (We shall look at this idea later.) If the element of miracle cannot be dismissed, the question of its meaning will have to be re-opened.

Miracle is thus not simply something unusual. A miracle is unusual, but not everything unusual is a miracle. The term can be

---

[2] See Chapter 14.
[3] Reginald H. Fuller, *Interpreting the Miracles*, London, S.C.M. Press, 1963, p. 20.

used in a flat sense, as more or less equivalent to 'the unusual'. But that is not its religious meaning. What is religious has to do with questions about the ultimate and about ultimate questions. Where miracle has religious significance it will be associated with man's questionings about ultimate meaning. It is not then simply or primarily an unusual event in the world of nature and history. It is an unusual event that is seen to have a bearing on the concern and question which man asks about his origin, meaning, ground and goal. A miraculous event in the religious sense is an event of unusual significance, bearing upon man's most serious and important questions about himself and his world. Only as this relation between the event and the question is seen is the claim made that God is revealed through the event. This we have seen to be the case in the three religions considered.

Judaism claimed that Yahweh had acted and revealed himself in the complex event of the Exodus. Yahweh called Moses and made him guide and leader of the slave people. Yahweh led the forefathers out of Egypt. Yahweh chose Israel and made his covenant with them. When the Hebrew asked questions, about his future, about the destiny of his people, about himself, his duty and his sin, he was pointed to the God who had been revealed in the Exodus. The event provided a focal point for the outlook of the Hebrew.

Similarly with Christianity. Meaning is given to the term 'God' by connecting it with a series of happenings, the decisive events in the first century, which go by the name Jesus Christ, or (as some writers call it) the Christ-event: the life, death, resurrection of Jesus and the faith that is grounded in these events.

In the cases considered the events are seen and understood to bear upon the human problem, to bring clarity to the nature of that problem and so fulfil the human concern.

The Christian claim is different from that made by the Hebrew, or by the Moslem, in that he (the Christian) gives a special status to his central figure, Jesus. He is more than a prophet.

In each of these cases we discern a pattern. Certain unusual events are interpreted as revealing God and in the appropriate response made to them, as providing the answer to the fundamental human questions.

The response of wonder (*miraculum* = wonder) is ingredient in the religious definition of miracle. To go back to our examples. The Exodus, the Hegira, the Resurrection may be explained on different levels. It is not true that one cannot offer an explanation at all.

For it is sometimes said that a miracle is such because it cannot be explained. In a sense this is true, since we explain an event by fitting it within the cause-effect network. Our quest for unity and tidiness does not rest until we can bring order into what appears disconnected, until we can find a place in the order of things for what puzzles us. But there are other kinds of explanation beside that kind which feels contented to have found a place for a problematic case in the cause-effect catena. To take an example. You can explain a letter by speaking of the physical components necessary to produce it, the composition of ink, the constitution of paper, the mechanics of pen movements, etc. That would be a fair enough explanation, if that is what was wanted.

One could explain the grammar of the sentences which composed it, or see it as an example of a certain style of composition, or of handwriting. Again under some conditions, that would be enough. But one might need to go further than that and take into account the purpose and the will which led to its being written, and the response with which it met on being received, opened and read. The letter might produce an answer to a real and specific human problem. 'Ah! Now I know where I stand! Now I know what decision I must take and what I must do!' The problem to which in such a case the letter provides the solution is a quite different one from that of the handwriting expert or of the postman. Explanations on the level of the latter have nothing to do with the resolve that initiated the writing nor with the response, say of surprised joy, with which it is received.

Since the religious explanation provides an answer to a different problem than does the cause-effect explanation, satisfactory and sufficient as this latter may be when it answers the problem to which it is seen to be appropriate, we shall not satisfactorily understand miracle unless we see it in the light of its religious purpose. It can be explained on other levels, of course. In the cases we have considered we would (probably, I suppose) ask the questions: What does the Exodus story tell us about leadership and mass movements? What does the resurrection reveal about the composition of narratives? What does the Hegira teach us about psychological response to failure? But these are not the questions the believer proposes he is answering. He claims that the stories shed light on the question of God and of man's quest for ultimate meanings, that when the proper response is made to them the ground has been laid for the answer to man's important questions, the 'crucial' questions.

Response to a happening or a series of happenings is decisive in assessing it as a miracle. If a certain kind of response is made there can be no talk of miracle. If another kind of response is made, there can. So there is the possibility of argument.

Imagine the following disagreement:

A child, given up to die by the doctors, makes a remarkable recovery. The believing mother says, 'It was a miracle.' The unbelieving father says, 'It was a remarkable coincidence.' The doctors say, 'We do not know how to explain it.'

To speak of the recovery as a miracle is a religious assessment, and as such the occasion for gratitude and the prayer of gratitude on the part of the one who makes it. The idea of miracle refers to certain special happenings which so to speak focus (and in focusing evoke) an attitude of wonder. It is not that one needs the marvellous, the stupendous, the unusual as one's daily religious diet, so that one's belief is maintained on such periodic injections of the marvellous and unusual. The important focal points are never simply marvellous or unusual. They are the occasions for a creative and not simply a marvellous wonder.

Miracle is a religious category. The response that is appropriate to miracle is a religious response. The idea of miracle is an example of what we might call a 'straddling' concept, that is one which can be treated on different levels of discourse because it has a reference within different realms of knowledge. If the scientist takes miracle as a kind of invasion into the order of nature then he might raise the question, 'What happens to the laws of nature when a miracle happens?' (*sotto voce,* 'if it ever should'). But, even if the believer is interested in giving an explanation so as to show that he is not unscientific in outlook, and that he has not overlooked important scientific questions, he knows that he is dealing primarily with a *religious* idea and experience. What is inexplicable on the level of science still has to be accounted for. That is a job theology does, namely to come to explicit understanding of the experience of faith. What might the theologian say in the case of miracle and the world in which it is claimed miracle takes place?

First, he might speak of God as Creator and the world as creation. This means that world is both dependent upon God and also has its own independence, its own order. This we saw in an earlier chapter.

Second, he might speak of the world as the plane upon which God is revealed and known. The world is like a stage upon which through the play and interplay of what goes on God may at times be seen and heard, and a response of wonder evoked. God's revelation is mediated. The medium for that revealing is the world and the process which takes place within it. These include human response.

Third, he might then speak of the need for being ready to respond, or of the importance of recognizing that you have already responded. He will have you try to recognize a level of experience and of undersanding other than that which is covered by a scientific explanation. He will refer you to a certain kind of experiencing.

Summary and Conclusion

Miracle stories are told with a purpose. We do not always have to believe that the details are factually true, but always have to ask what the purpose of the story is. A religious community points to unusual events at its beginning. In the case of Christianity it is the resurrection of Jesus, which it is claimed has a bearing upon the ultimate questions human beings ask. Indeed that the event constitutes a revelation of God, as it is claimed do similarly crucial events in other religions. Response of an appropriate kind to the event is to be included in the definition of miracle.

Discussion Questions

What happened at the Exodus of the Hebrews from Egypt?

Is it true that your perspective makes a difference to what you see? Where do perspectives come from? How are they changed? For example, how does a religious attitude emerge? Why do some believers become agnostic?

8 | What is Nonsense?

SOMETIMES you have to say things so simply that you're sorry that you don't have more time to explain. At other times you have so much time to explain that a question that was asked or a comment that was made as a statement to end statements can be dealt with at considerable length. In the former case it's difficult if you want to explain more. In the second case it's trying for the listener because he thinks that the pronouncing of a sentence is enough to close the matter, whereas he finds that if you talk to him about the question for—let's say—twenty weeks, he's got more than he bargained for. Not that that always makes a difference.

Josephine, sitting at the back of the form, asked the teacher in the course of a class in World Religions why the Christian talked about God as three in one. The teacher said a few sentences about God being revealed to human beings in three ways (and all sorts of heresy lurk behind that kind of statement, as the theologians will well know) to which he received the reply, 'What a lot of nonsense!'

Mary, sitting in the circle of a discussion group, let the leader of the group say a few sentences about the problem they intended to discuss, Science and Religion, and then provided her contribution in the form of the comment which if true was supposed to close off the discussion for good. 'I'm studying science. We deal with facts. Religion is a matter of feeling. Nonsense.'

These are very good sorts of statements to make. On one condition. That they be talked about. Indeed the problem of the meaningfulness of religious statements has been talked about at great length and sometimes with much good sense. But we cannot get anywhere if someone says 'Shut-up' by waving the notion of nonsense in front of us. I would like to think that the word 'nonsense' is a guaranteed way of protracting the discussion: with profit if we're really serious. If what religious people say is nonsense then the quicker they are convinced of it the better. But it is very unlikely that the pronouncing of the word will be enough to produce the conviction.

When then can we say with justification: 'That is nonsense!'? Since the assertion may be a cloak for ignorance or obscurantism, we shall consider its meaning rather closely.

First, to look at a rather technical meaning the word might assume. We speak of the five senses: sight, taste, touch, hearing, smell. When we see something we usually know what it is we see. We say that seeing is believing. If we see somebody somewhere we know that he was there. When we say so our word is testimony and our testimony is accepted. But there are important claims we make of which we cannot say in any non-metaphorical sense, 'I saw it' or 'I heard it' or the like. The believer neither sees nor hears God, in the straightforward sense of these sense terms. God is not directly available to the believer as the result of some sense-experience.

There are two interesting questions to be raised at this point. Should knowledge derived from sense-experience be given some privileged status over other claims to knowledge: e.g. from some 'intuition' (I know that it is wrong to steal!)? Is all knowledge derived from sense-experience?

If the answer to both of these questions be 'yes!', then it would seem impossible for religious claims to be given due consideration. Since the knowledge such claims involve is not derived from sense-experience, those claims would in a quite specific meaning be nonsense. But would anyone, even David Hume, really believe that all knowledge is derived from some experience of sense? He himself admitted, after composing a lengthy treatise on the problem of human knowledge, to a 'philosophical melancholy and delirium' which could only be cured by dining, playing backgammon or by some merriment with his friends.

The term 'Nonsense!' used as an objection to religious claims customarily means 'not sensible'; that is, not intelligible, not capable of being given an intelligible meaning. This may mean one of two things:

(a) I can't understand it!
(b) It can't be understood.

Religion and Science

Of course (*b*) includes (*a*). If something is incomprehensible, then neither I nor you nor anyone else will be able to understand it. (*b*) includes (*a*) by definition. Sometimes when one is making the objection 'That is nonsense' he is hoping to get the hearer to move from (*a*) to (*b*). 'I can't understand it' really implies, you know (since you are aware that I am intelligent, balanced, etc.), 'It can't be understood'. But one must be careful that this is not a trick. It may be true that 'I can't understand it' is due to the fact that 'It can't be understood'. But it may not.

Let us start with the case of esoteric knowledge. In the case of very particularized knowledge there may be only four or five people alive who could understand it. Notice that this does not necessarily have to be an erudite knowledge. Perhaps only a few people hold a quite simple secret, know a language, a code or a script unknown to anyone else. Only when esoteric knowledge is communicated does it become intelligible.

So, in the instance of a secret society, the purpose is not *necessarily* to produce highly sophisticated knowledge and ideas, but rather to keep whatever ideas and practices it has to itself. The member is thus privileged in that he belongs, and in that he can know what the outsider cannot know, what the ideas and practices are and what they mean. So someone looking on may see nothing, but the initiate may see significance in the secret signs or in the special words. In a case like this then, 'I can't understand it' may simply mean, 'I haven't been initiated into the secrets'. In the case of extremely sophisticated erudition it might mean 'I do not have the capacity to grasp it'. So a set of equations which Einstein would easily have understood would be nonsense in this sense to the high-school pupil, just as a diary in Sanskrit would be to a young English child. It is not beyond comprehension, but it is still nonsense—to them.

The process of becoming mature involves the coming to understand what one did not understand before. How does one come to understand? How is understanding broadened? If one is confronted with what appears to him to have little or no meaning, yet which is claimed to be of some importance, how does he come to the place where he begins to understand, and to agree as to the importance?

1. Think. Draw on your resources. Tap your experience. Attempt

What is Nonsense?

to co-ordinate what you already understand or what you think you are beginning to understand.

2. Broaden your experience. You will have read about the experiences of other people, and seen them at second hand, so to speak. You can draw lines to your own experience, make analogies and apply them. Where possible and worth-while you might seek the experiences which will put you in a position of advantage and enable you to see what you could not see before. As life goes on the sensitive openness to different experiences which it brings will widen the scope of one's appreciation, enabling one to understand what before was obscure.

For example, we may have been orphaned when young, and read about the delights of parenthood. But the idea will not mean much to us. We will not be able to deny that it is a meaningful idea to other people, when they stop to give it thought. But it may be only when life has come the circle to the time of our own parenthood that we shall really be able to enter into the understanding of the meaning of the term. How can one really understand the meaning 'orphan' without having been one? How can one understand the responsibilities of being, let us say, the President of the United States, without having been one? How can one understand poverty if one has never been poor? How can one understand the claims that God is a Father, if one has never had a good father? Indeed how does one understand what is meant when people talk about God? or religious faith? or revelation?

Let us take an example from an Eastern religion, from Zen Buddhism. Zen is a religion of contemplation within which the guidance of a master is considered essential to the disciple's progress. The development of the novice depends upon the relation between himself and his master, who will give him problems, puzzles of a most enigmatic kind to work on. These are called koans. They seem to be meaningless. For example, 'What noise does one hand make?' 'A girl is crossing the street. Is she the younger or the older sister?' Puzzles such as these were kept secret for many centuries, but the interesting thing is that when they became available together with the answers nobody took much interest in them. When the secret formulae, questions and answers were made known without the master-novice relationship, they had really lost their meaning. Outside the context of the discipline

Religion and Science

which the novice sought, and of the experience of the master who sought to guide and awaken the novice, they had little application. They were meaningless without a particular experience and a particular community.

For the fact is that experiences can be shared and only as some things are experienced together can they be experienced at all. In a genuine community the members can understand one another because they have common interests and experiences. They are willing to submit at times to the judgement of the community in preference to their own, since they may feel that their experience has not been extensive enough to enable them to make confidently the kind of judgement that is demanded. Such submission happens constantly in many different ways in the scientific community; in the school, college and university; in the political community; in the religious community.

The problem of understanding another community, or a member of another community has its basis in the difference of experience that lies between us. Where we have not shared the history of another individual or community, it becomes a problem to share his perspectives.

Now, the Christian religion belongs to and is found within the Christian community, which claims a shared history, and a sharing of a present experience. This links us with talk about revelation.

Summary and Conclusion

It seems easy to dismiss religion as nonsense until one tries to find out what the objection means. The believer claims that his faith can be understood. We increase our understanding by expanding our experience or by thinking further about what we have experienced. When our experience is the shared experience of a particular community it may take a genuine effort of imagination and of will to avoid prejudice and to show sympathetic understanding.

Discussion Questions

Can one know that something one does not understand is not nonsense but intelligible? If so, how?

What is Nonsense?

How do you make a distinction between what you do not understand now but might come to understand, and what you do not understand and could not (at any time) understand?

Attempt a definition of *prejudice*. Find and document specific examples. Discuss the causes and the remedies.

Is it possible to be impartial? Should one be impartial?

Is one impartial if one makes allowance for one's prejudices?

How does one allow for the perspective from which one sees things?

9 | *What is Religion?*

INTELLECTUAL growth is bound to bring confusion, doubt and uncertainty. When we move from the relatively simple statements and definitions which we learnt, before the age of abstract thinking came, to the more sophisticated qualifications which we had not been ready to consider previously, it appears that what we learned then is not only over-simple but indeed wrong. Press any reality, and you'll find it's not quite as simple as it appeared.

In the protracted learning process that stretches from infancy to adulthood an important aspect is the unlearning of the simple. This involves coming to see that what we once learned was an over-simplification, a convenient fiction used for pedagogical purposes.

So we were taught that light moves in straight lines, only to have to relearn that when we started to be told about light waves. We were taught that Boyle's Laws were gospel truth, then as we grew older we were exposed to the deviations from these gas laws. When we were introduced to the theory of electrons we were provided with the picture of spheres moving around, only later when mature to learn about wave mechanics. We thought once that the orbits of the planets were elliptical, but later found out that the matter was much more complex than that, as we did about what we had been taught concerning the atom and its clusters of units.

It would be foolish to remain with the simplicity we had been taught when, older and ready to understand the complexities, we came to realize that if we probed deeper there was much more to it than we had been able earlier to grasp. Now when things get complicated people get discouraged. Their effort or their interest lags or both. Press any aspect of reality and it's more complicated than it at first seems. It's then that if we're serious we shall have to persevere—and only if we do will we get anywhere near an adequate understanding of the matter in view.

What is Religion?

One of the too simple ideas about religion is that it is believing. Faith is involved in religion, but religion is not simply believing something, or believing in something. The kind of faith that is religious is involved faith, which is the response to a concern that touches the very root of man's being. That is, it is faith of a certain kind.

Believing that intelligent persons will not be content with secondary sources of information in discussing the question of religion, but will want primary and authentic information, let us ask, 'How can you find out what religion is?'

Let us suppose someone who did not know asked you 'What is dancing?' There would be various ways you could try to make clear to him the meaning of the word. You will first describe the activity involved in terms which he already understood, for example, you could talk of rhythmic movements of hands and feet according to pattern and tempo. Second, you could draw pictures, or show him photographs, pointing to the relevant parts of the pictures as you attempted a description. The picture would be a symbol that would assist your verbal explanations. The third line to be taken would be to do a dance in front of him and say 'This is dancing'. You could take him to many places where different kinds of dancing were done in various contexts and say, 'Look, that is dancing!' Would you really have conveyed to him what dancing is, if you were not able to persuade him to participate in the activity in some way or other? You could say, 'Come, put you feet like this and your hands likes this and listen to the beat, and go, go, go! Now you are dancing.' If then he wished to know more about it, perhaps more than you are able to tell him, you would advise him to read books, or to go to a teacher or school of dance.

Back to our question: 'What is religion—how would you find out?' First, you could listen to people who write and talk about it competently. You will have to remember (and I'm sorry to have to say this) that the most sincere people will not always be the most helpful, and the most obvious people may not give you the greatest help. Consider various descriptions of what religion is from different sources. Consider the various symbols that are used in presenting the religion. In other words, build up an impression from descriptions and symbols. Second, you could go to where religion is claimed to be in evidence, and take note of the evidence. Where

Religion and Science

there are many kinds of the phenomenon, as in the case of dancing and religion, you will then proceed to make certain generalizations.

A generalization is a statement which applies to many instances by specifying common features of the particular instances, which in many other respects may well be different. Scientific laws are generalizations. They are intended to have a general application, for example, the law of inertia. Certain particular features, or one particular feature are abstracted from the total situation so as to make a general statement about many situations.

One way of trying to find out what religion is is by noting the common features in the different instances of what claims to be religion. But we meet here with certain very real problems. The first is that what appear to be common features between religions may, with closer and more careful attention, turn out only to be superficial resemblances, in some cases to be quite different phenomena. Let us try a generalization: Religion is belief in God and devotion to him. Two considerations spring to mind. Is Buddhism, or Confucianism, a religion then? Neither have an explicit belief in 'God'. Moreover does the generalization 'God' really help us in learning about what religion is? After all G-O-D is an English word and each religion has its own name for the object of its devotion, e.g. Yahweh, Allah, Vishnu, Brahma. If we start with a generalization we soon begin to qualify it, that is to 'de-generalize' it. But if we insist that we stick with generalizations we shall have to replace the term 'God' with a term of wider generalization, for example 'higher power'. But by doing this we then let in other phenomena and ideas which do not at first appear to be religious. This all leaves us with a question, whether the observer's way, the way of holding religions at a distance so as to define (while quite legitimate an exercise) really puts us on to real religion, or only lets us see religion as a phenomenon, or as a series of phenomena.

The second problem is that in making a generalization we must be sure to include everything that should be included. On some definitions Buddhism and Confucianism would not qualify as religions. But assuming that they are examples of the phenomena in which we are interested our definition will have to include them. It appears that we will have to try out different definitions. We will have to make an initial procedural assumption, namely that

What is Religion?

what claims or purports to be religious be taken into consideration as an example relevant to our inquiry. Shuffling motions may turn out to be a dance! Out of this process of comparison will emerge the realization that there are persistent features across the different religions, and also the difficulty of reducing these data to a simple formula.

Let us try another line. In all of our inquiry we are assuming that we have 'some idea', as we say, of what we're looking for. So let us look now at the individual and ask, 'When is a person religious?' What are the characteristics and attitudes which a religious person will exemplify? The signs may not be obvious ones. Religious people are not always labelled. Moreover we shall find, as in our previous investigation, that there is plenty of variety to occupy our interest. Perhaps we shall run into the same difficulties if we try to generalize as we did before. But the question 'When is a person religious?' is not an empty one and we must try to give some answer to it. Notice that this need not be the same sort of question as the previous one. If one were to answer, 'An individual is religious when he is a member of a religious community', we would be back to the previous kind of answer, where we tried to specify significant features of the community in relation to other such communities. A short cut would be to settle for one such community and maintain that it provided the norm for all judgements of a religious kind. If the range of our knowledge is limited to an inadequate knowledge of only one tradition we are not exactly in a commanding position to make rational judgements! But we must begin where we are and the way to make the best of it is to start with the knowledge and the experience we have: seeking satisfaction but not becoming self-satisfied with it, like the parson in *Tom Jones* who when he talked of religion meant Christianity, and when he talked of Christianity meant Protestantism, and when he talked of Protestantism meant the Church of England.

If the question about the individual is not to be subsumed under that of the community, we must look at some tell-tale features of the individual as a religious person, of individual piety. There will be plenty of variety here and plenty of room for differing evaluations and for different sorts of evaluations. Are there any particular characteristics which manifest themselves in the life of the individual which are distinctly religious by which the phenomenon 'religion' may be recognized?

There are some forms of religion which lay the greatest stress on the state, attitudes and feelings of the individual, speaking of the need for the person to realize his selfhood. The guidance given for the achievement of this end may be very detailed. In religions of law for example rules are provided to cover every detail of life—almost. Guidance may be very vague, as in some contemplative religions where the individual is left to care for his soul solo, where he must work out his salvation on his own. But whatever sort of guidance, tight or loose, religion provides in the way of direction for the individual believer, at some point the believer himself decides for himself. First, in making the religious commitment and then that such a commitment is best nurtured and maintained in one particular tradition rather than another, that one form of piety exemplified in some particular religious community best expresses his own feelings on the matter. It is a good question whether there is such a thing as an entirely individual religion, namely one in which the subject is entirely alone, doing something in his solitude. But that does not mean that we may not focus upon the individual and ask what shows up in his religious experience.

There is no *one* frame of mind which may be said to be religious to the exclusion of all others. Using the old three-fold formula of intellect, feeling and will, we have to say that religion is not a particular mode of feeling, nor a particular way of willing, nor a particular way of thinking. Each of these is present in the total experience of the religious person, and to emphasise one at the expense of the others is to distort the reality and the description. Religion involves the whole man, in many and varied activities and frames of mind.

We said earlier that religion is not simply to believe, not even to believe in God. 'I believe in God, so what?' is a possible question. The epistle of James speaks of the devils who believe and tremble! Believing certain things is always present in religion: but it is not religion. 'Concern' is more fundamental than belief. Belief[1] as distinct from faith is assent on the basis of evidence, to a proposition or to a set of propositions. Religion is not the acceptance of the truth of propositions on the basis of evidence.

[1] See Chapter 15.

Such is an over-intellectualizing, and intellectualistic distortion, of faith.

Such over-intellectualization does not have to be at all sophisticated. There is the intellectualism of the postcard creed as well as of the theological system. The propositions believed may be very simple indeed. They may be rather complicated. At the many and varied levels of sophistication we speak of intellectualization when belief, acceptance of the propositions, or the scheme of propositions is emphasized at the expense of commitment of a whole-souled and personal kind.

'Concern' in contrast implies the involvement of the feelings and the will in the problem and its answer. The whole person is involved in the decision to be taken. Of course the intellect is involved. Faith is reasonable but is not solely an act of the reason. It is the concerned act of the total person.

Religious concern is concern of a special kind. Later we shall think of concern about the future, and about the past, but at present we shall ask what sort of concern the religious concern is, on what level it appears.

To do this we can think about different ways of asking questions. There are some questions soon answered, asked for the sake of information which can easily be supplied. Let us call these 'trivial' questions. There are other questions which require research and persistence but which, if the appropriate attitudes are present, are amenable to an answer. Let us call these 'research' questions. There is another kind of question. There are questions which keep coming back, demanding renewal of answers which we once gave, or revision of the old answers. They come back time and again, generation after generation, and can't be settled like the trivial and the research questions. We shall call these the 'perennial' questions. They are concerned questions. You feel yourself involved in the answer that is or is to be given. There is an urgency about getting that answer, however long you may have to wait. The question just does not go away. It persists. It is about life itself. Such questions when they ask about the whole of human life, about its origin, its ground and its goal are religious questions. Because they ask about the meaning of life itself they are fundamental and ultimate questions. Religion is that kind of concern which relates to such ultimate questions.

There is a context in which such questions are asked. It is the incompleteness of human life. Every religion diagnoses the human condition and finds that there is something wrong with it. It proposes a remedy for the condition. To those who share the concern, which means 'feeling' as well as 'seeing' the problem, both the emotion and the intellect being involved, the proposed diagnosis makes sense. This means 'feeling' as well as 'seeing' the solution as a solution to the problem which has been felt and seen. They 'experience' the condition and follow the diagnosis of it. To them the proffered remedy has real meaning. The concern is now directed, and unity, wholeness is given to life. Integration takes place in the midst of human life, individual and social.

When we move from a general definition of religion to specific religions, we find that there we must talk of commitment to specific beliefs; to particular concepts of God, or the ultimate; to specific ways of defining the human problem and its solution; to particular rituals, myths and explanations.

This brings us to our third element, that of the will. Action is involved in the finding and the putting into effect of a solution. The will is involved in such action of directing the personality in the requisite channels. Appropriate attitudes are willed and chosen, even if when it's done the believer says that the willing and the choosing were not altogether of his own doing, using some such term as 'grace' or 'gift'. Indeed the concern and the attitude must sometimes be willed when one would want to escape. But it is always they which give filling to the will. Something is willed. That something is already a claim which can be accepted or refused. This act of choosing is the function of the will.

Particular religions differ in what they propose for this content. Every religion tells its stories, thinks its thoughts, raises its problems, performs its rituals in different ways. But in that religion is a human concern, over and over again the same themes are dealt with, the themes raised in the perennial questions of mankind: What sort of being is man? How should we treat one another? What is ultimate, where and how is the ultimate known? What is he (it) like? How does God show up and make his will known? What is the being and origin of the universe? What of the future?

Each proposes a way of answering these questions, of man, of ethics, of God, of revelation, of world and of the future. The

What is Religion?

way of religion is to answer the questions on a fundamental level and to propose that you can live by the answer given.

Summary and Conclusion

In defining religion we can examine religions as phenomena and make generalizations about them. We can also look at the individual and ask what a religious person is like. In doing both of these we learn that religion is a concern by a man about the ultimate ground and goal of his being, and a specific commitment of faith in the light of that concern.

Discussion Questions

How would you make clear to someone who did not know what the following expressions mean:

        Music   Pure Water
        Money   Celebration
        Fruit   Flower?

What do we mean by the expressions 'the penny drops'? 'the light dawns'? Are there kinds of knowledge where you have to do something in order to know (e.g. look, listen, set aside preconceptions, keep awake, make a formal agreement 'for the sake of argument', go to a certain place at a certain time, etc.)? Are there kinds of knowledge which, so to speak, come as a flash?

What could you communicate in the following ways:

        Giving an example   Naming
        Telling how a term is used Classifying
        Showing a picture   Pointing
        Describing   Demonstrating?

If you wanted to know what 'science', 'religion' was, what would you do?

How would you communicate the meaning of the following to a person whose language you did not understand (and who did not understand yours)? Would you have to have anything in common to do so?

Sleep
Water
Don't do that!
I believe I can trust you.

10 | Interaction

THIS chapter makes and illustrates one point. How we think about science will influence how we think about religion. How we think about religion will influence how we think about science. Changes in thinking about science are accompanied by changes in thinking about religion. Changes in thinking about religion are accompanied by changes in thinking about science.

Modern science grew up in the West, in Christian countries. It is an interesting fact that many of the leading scientists in that century of genius, the eighteenth, were Christian and many of these were clergymen. Some had difficulty in getting together their thinking about science and religion and were aware of tensions, even contradictions in their thought. But more of that in a moment. The fact is that modern science grew up in a milieu that was congenial to an understanding of the world. The Judaeo-Christian tradition taught that the world was real. The body was real. Both were good. This belief in the reality and the goodness of the world provided the right conditions for the systematic exploration of the world and its methodological understanding, which we now call by the name of science. The matter-of-fact concreteness, the down-to-earth-ness of the Hebrews ensured that wherever that culture spread there would be a joy in the world and in the body: were these not the creation of God?

It was in the East that the idea grew up that the world was an illusion, that existence in the body was a limitation, that the way of salvation was in escaping from the body and from the world on to another level or into another form of existence. It follows that if the world is an illusion we ought to try to escape it, to try to find peace in some trans-worldly state, some nirvana where the unreality of the body and of the world are escaped. The conditions were not right for a devotion to the systematic understanding of the world. The following chart illustrates the point.

SCIENCE ← understand it ← real good ← is ← { WORLD / UNIVERSE / NATURE }
→ is an illusion → escape it → NIRVANA

The affirmation that provided the favourable context for the development of science was a religious one.

As science began to develop within that context, and began to provide new images for the understanding of that nature which had before been directly connected with religious modes of thinking, problems of co-ordination arose that had not presented themselves before. The efforts of generations were directed to trying to think together the new categories of the physical science of Newton (for example) and the convictions of the Christian community. Newton was a Christian.

It came to be understood that more and more explanations of the processes of nature could be given which had no need to speak about God as, in any sense, cause. As such *secular* explanations were given the possibility of a new atheism arose, a methodological atheism. For the purposes of scientific explanation the idea of God had no place. Where he had been called in to complete the incomplete explanation (as well as his counterpart the Devil and the demons) new answers were now given. Eventually it came to be realized that the Christian must share this methodological atheism with everyone else engaged in the scientific enterprise.

This is so well expressed in the oft-told story of Laplace that it bears repetition. Napoleon asked Laplace why God was not mentioned in his book (*Celestial Mechanics*), to which Laplace gave the reply, 'Sir, I have no need of *that* hypothesis'. What he meant was that in a mechanistic hypothesis of the stability of the Solar System God had no function. This did not mean that the scientific explanation had rendered the idea of God untenable, say as Creator or Sustainer. It meant that for the purposes of a particular kind of explanation, the concept of God (in this case as intervening to prevent the universe slipping into chaos) was irrelevant.

So a new problem arose for the believer, with his religious convictions—to co-ordinate indubitable certainties about truth drawn from different areas of experience. In the language we have been using earlier on in this book, his problem was to co-ordinate different levels of explanation, giving to each its rightful place, not of banning it. It was a matter, and often a painful one, of specifying what that rightful place was, marking out its boundaries, and fighting off opponents who were convinced that there should be no territory at all.

Now, since Newton and his disciples were Christian, they attempted to co-ordinate what they took for certainties, namely, that God was the Creator of the world-universe; that the world, etc., was a universe, that is that there was one set of laws that could be applied throughout (this was Galileo's achievement); that the proper way of conceiving this universe was on the analogy of a machine. If we added a fourth to these, it would be the conviction that miracles took place in this 'closed system'.

The way the eighteenth century thought about science affected its religious thought. Since the idea of mechanism, and of the universe as a vast machine, was *the* model, that imagery was in due course employed in the service of theology. A fine illustration of the intricate, predictable, and continuous working of a machine was provided for the nonce by such a clock as had been constructed for the city of Strasbourg. The clock, or the watch, provided a most useful piece of illustration for the Christian thinker and apologist. God as creator was thought of as the machine-maker. He was like the clock-maker. But he was such a clock-maker that once the clock had been constructed, it would then go of its own accord without any interference from its maker, the clock, of course, being the world. However, in an extreme case the clockmaker-God may have to bestir himself, screwdriver in hand, and initiate something that would not otherwise have taken place. But that was only in time of dire emergency. In this way the Deists (people who believed in an absentee landlord sort of God) felt that they could co-ordinate the three important convictions into a viable harmony: God created in the beginning; the universe is a vast machine whose laws can be discovered and elaborated by the newly emerged scientific method; the occurrence of miracles as part of the Christian tradition.

A new sort of defence for Christianity was now proposed. Look at items within the world, aspects of the world as parts of the machine, as evidence of design. The human eye was a stock illustration. Just as a machine implies a machine-maker, so do the evidences of design within the world imply a Grand Architect, a Great Designer of the world. The new science seemed to provide rich and compelling analogies for the Christian apologist, and the exciting discovery that nature's laws, once 'hid in night' were now becoming open to the day was made even more compelling by the idea that the advances were congenial to the understanding of Christian faith, that the scientist was perhaps even 'thinking God's thoughts after him'.

Time passed. The process of secularization went on. Was God really needed as a principle of explanation? That was the question which forced itself upon minds which, in spite of their desire to retain the idea of God in some form or other as an explanatory device, had to admit conflict and problem at the outset, and later to resolve the issues by admitting that God was not a principle of scientific explanation, however conceived. You cannot at the same time have a Deistic God (in order to get the whole thing going) who stands apart from things, and a God within the machine (call him 'spirit' or something like it) who maintains it. If mechanism is a scientific principle, it will show itself to be such by its extensibility: its capacity to explain more and more.

God was seen to be less and less of a principle of explanation. This being so the question became more and more pertinent: 'What could he explain or be the explanation of?' In contrast to the extensibility of certain important concepts used in science, the concept of God, in view of the expanding knowledge, has had its range of applicability more and more restricted in relation to the growing sciences.

This was a particular problem for those scientists who were Christian. They realized that they had to find a way of harmonizing faith in God and that it implied with the concepts and hypotheses which they were developing in their scientific work. This led to conflicts which they had to find a way of resolving. In some cases it meant that their private mind did not always correspond to their public image. A case in point is that of the Swedish botanist Carl Linnaeus (1707–78).

Linnaeus was the great classifier of the eighteenth century. Using the schema of genera and species, he attempted to name and to classify every known botanical specimen. He also was Christian. For theological reasons he accepted, at the outset as a working principle, the notion of the fixity of species. Was it not Christian doctrine that when God created the world, he created a set number of species? The interesting point is that this teaching, which is now called the doctrine of 'special creation', was the outcome of thinking about God as Creator in terms of the idea of species, which was a relatively new idea. To think of the Creator God as having prepared a certain number of species at the beginning requires that one has the idea of species to begin with. This is a modern idea and not an ancient one. Once the idea has been sounded, a re-interpretation of the less explicit ancient doctrine of creation held in the early centuries of the Christian church could take place. It was thought to be *required* by those who accepted both that God is creator and the scheme of classification according to genera and species. For the record, Linnaeus later came to doubt the idea of fixity of species and so represents the divided mind of the eighteenth century. But our point has been made. The way you think about religion has influence upon the way you think about science, and vice-versa.

We have seen that advance in scientific knowledge and the creation of scientific theory and hypotheses has had its influence upon Christian thinking. There are a limited number of possible responses to the presence of a new and continuously expanding knowledge which seems to have a bearing upon beliefs held in religion. These may be divided into two types: those which do not and those which do welcome new knowledge, which see it as a threat or as an opportunity. The labels conservative and liberal respectively, traditionalist and modernist respectively, are sometimes put to these two classes. The difference is a fundamental one—a matter of outlook, or attitude and of principle. There are two classes within each type.

A.   The traditionalist type comprises:

   1. those who ignore the new explorations or the new truth;
   2. those who oppose it.

B.   The liberal type comprises:

   3. those who explore but do not co-ordinate;
   4. those who explore and who attempt to co-ordinate.

Religion and Science

1 and 2 represent variants of the attitude of entrenchment, 3 and 4 variants of the attitude of exploration.

A says, We have the truth and we know it. We also know the dangers of departing from the truth we know (rather vague about that though). We must be sure that people in our community do not hear about what might disturb them. We must in the name of faith and of the defence of the truth shield them and ourselves from new (=modern) and disturbing ideas. *A* attempts this in one of two ways. In the case of 1, the attempt is made to act as if the ideas had not come into being. For anyone of such a religious bent who lives in a modern world, made such by the application of science to life, that's most difficult to carry through with any consistency. Transportation isn't what it used to be, nor is the structure and the content of our houses, and the knowledge and technique of our surgeons. The believer participates in these benefits and multitudes of other examples of scientific culture. But in religion *A* 1 tries to avoid the new knowledge and the impact it could make upon his belief.

2 mounts two main methods of attack. Either he fights the 'modern' enterprises on principle, the principle being that it is damaging to the faith and disturbing to the community of faith, or he engages in conflict on particular issues which he feels to be a particular threat of danger, such as the creation-evolution question, or the problem of the authority of the Bible.

Both lead to obscurantism and the protective mentality—'We must keep the community pure from the dangers of modernism!' 'We must not let the acids of modernity eat out the fundamentals of the faith delivered to the saints.'

We move now to *B*, where an interesting difference shows itself on the part of those willing to explore modern knowledge.

3 is the way of the two compartments. One is kept for science and one for religion, the twain, like East and West, never meeting. A sophisticated scientist and a naïve believer, one and the same person, may at the same time have a wide open mind for his science and a rather firmly closed one for his religion. In any case the contents of the two bags are not seen to be compatible or incompatible because they are never opened and looked at at the same time in the same place. They are two worlds, two languages, two minds.

Interaction

4 represents the desire and effort at both exploration and co-ordination. It assumes a reasonably adequate knowledge from the two spheres. It holds the conviction that all truth is one and that therefore you should try to grasp and to express its unity. Where this unity does not appear, there is a problem—something sticks out (that's what the word problem means) and has to be looked at.

1 and 2 refuse to entertain problems with any real seriousness. 3 is willing to shelve them. 4 is prepared to live with them and is ready to doubt and to question, assuming that truth lies in front and not all behind, that truth must be striven for.

Life is then a quest.

Summary and Conclusion

Science grew up in the West where the belief was held that the world was real and good. As scientific explanations were given, God became a problem and a new sort of atheism arose where one was convinced of the truth of science and of God as creator, a process of rethinking became necessary in order to hold the two together. When confronted with truth from different sources, various attitudes of mind show themselves; conservatives entrench, liberals explore.

Discussion Questions

Find specific examples of ways in which a religious outlook influences perspectives in areas of activity and thought.

What perspectives on the world, on human life, would make a religious attitude impossible?

Discover ways in which the theory of evolution, or the theory of relativity has had influence on Christian theology.

What is the difference between liberalism and conservatism in Christian theology? Find examples.

11 | Science and the Future

THE history of modern science has been one of progressive control over nature. Science has learned *how* to manipulate and the results have been astonishing. The dedicated scientist, devoting his life and talent to the understanding of the world, has made possible a knowledge undreamed of by the ancients or the medievals. He has provided a competence and a power to this modern age which none other has had. The researcher may be interested in research and discovery for its own sake, and feel that his task is complete when the project which he has set for himself has issued in success, when he has learned the *how*, when what was not previously known has been dscovered. The scientist is not, as scientist, interested in what will happen after the know-how and the knowledge passes out into the common fund, for use by human beings in human relationships.

For, of course, the *application* of the know-how to the many and varied walks of human life, wherever it is thought to produce benefit or advantage, does inevitably take place. It is the process of applying the know-how and the results that this produces that the achievements of the scientist get beyond him, out of his control. He may have been responsible for initial discoveries. He may have no idea of the use to which what he has discovered will be put. He is not a prophet, after all. There have been cases of scientists who, deeply regretting the uses to which knowledge for which they were responsible have been put, have confessed their utter disillusionment and bitterness. They would not have laboured as they did, had they known what would have happened after them.

The story of Alfred Nobel provides an example.

After continued researches he produced an explosive 'safer' than nitro-glycerine, namely dynamite. He patented it and it was soon in production by arms manufacturers all over the world. He hoped for its peaceful use in road-building, mining, building tunnels.

Indeed he claimed, 'The knowledge of these high explosives would remove the danger of future conflicts by making mankind realize how destructive war had become.' His optimism was not to be realized. He not only had to contend with his own disappointment at the harmful employment of his product but also with a wave of popular feeling which rose against him. It was after reading a damning 'obituary' of himself in the newspapers, that he decided he must try to do something for the cause of peace. So he endowed what we now know as the Nobel Prize.

Another case in point is that of Oppenheimer whose refusal to head the research programme in atomic energy in the United States after the use of the bomb on Hiroshima and Nagasaki was an ethical decision which he felt he had to make.

In both of these cases we have the scientist facing the problem of what he ought to do as a human being in the world of non-scientists, in the personal, social and political world.

The opening decades of the twentieth century saw the invention and introduction of devices hitherto unknown. For the first time wireless telegraphy became a reality, the internal combustion engine was adapted for mass production in the motor car, the first flight across the English Channel took place, then there and back, then across the Atlantic. Advances were made in the knowledge of disease, of explosives, of weapons. Someone said that the possession of one machine gun at Waterloo would have decided the day for the side which had it! In due course these (and other) achievements were applied to human purposes, one of which unfortunately consists in the effort at the wholesale slaughter of human beings. So the Second World War was different from every other war in history. In many ways, of course, but our interest is to point out that scientific endeavour and achievement are directed to particular areas of human interest and activity.

This means that we inherit problems, and multiply problems, which we would never have to face but for the understanding and achievements of science. For example, the possibility of germ-warfare presupposes expert knowledge in many fields, not the least in biology. There would be no possibility of germ-warfare were not a whole and magnificent set of accomplishments of many generations, not the least our own, at our disposal. The application of the accumulated knowledge of science of generations to the terrifying

Religion and Science

task of biological destruction is only one example of how the initial aims, or the initial neutrality of the scientist can be quite overlaid with sinister, non-scientific purposes.

But there is another aspect of the application of science to life. The contemporary woman in the West, whose husband earns a reasonable income, can have brought to her kitchen and her home the products of a sophisticated technology, which has made her life quite different from that of her Victorian great-grandmother. There seems no end of the products put out for her convenience, and as production outstrips consumer demand, it may be necessary to create 'needs' to keep the economy stable. This raises the further problem: the problem of manufacture. Who is to control the directions which production takes? Is profit to be the one consideration? Or is the proliferation of goods produced to be subject to no control, to become like a frolic, as it has been pictured. The difference between a dance and a frolic, is that the dance is (or used to be) controlled and predictable! It followed a pattern, and was ordered—as to the frolic, who knows how it will end?

The scientific know-how at his disposal enables the manufacturer to produce almost whatever he thinks will be profitable. The process of production becomes uncontrolled and perhaps even uncontrollable, in brief—a frolic! Is the only pattern to be found in the gratification of the narrow-minded selfishness of those who stand to make profit, or is there some long-term benefit that will ensue?

Since we have now raised the question of control, let us consider it under two aspects. The point we shall make is that the question of control which is inevitably raised by the application of science to human activity and interests is *not a scientific question*. We look, then, at two forms of the question of control:

1. The control of 'man' by 'Man'. We were naturally appalled by the reports of 'experiments' on human beings in concentration camps. We feel that there is a basic respect due to the body of man, and that no other human being has a right to abuse that body. The question of the consent of the 'patient' or 'guinea pig' is another one, to which we can only allude here. But if, for example, it has been decided that techniques in germ warfare must be developed, there comes a point where human beings must be used to test the

products. The Pentagon has employed volunteers, who are conscientious objectors, for this purpose. They were asked to volunteer for dangerous work, but did not know exactly what that meant: perhaps death, paralysis, or worse still in some cases, the effect would not be known for years.

We shall control the controllers, may be a contemporary way of translating the old question: *'Quis custodiet ipsos custodes?'* For the *controller* and the *controlled* present us with two quite different images of man: the almighty, white-coated medical scientist and the patient waiting upon some word of hope, some new formula, or some new experiment, perhaps on himself!

2. The control of man in relation to his environment. We have of late had forced upon us, and repeatedly, the concern for the keeping of the world in which we live fit to keep us living in it. The waters which surround us, the atmosphere we breathe, the land upon which we depend for our sustenance just can't be treated without a certain constraint, *if* we want to maintain healthy human life upon the planet. At least we must ask a less narrowly selfish question about the environment if we wish to survive. We have to consider the long-term effects of our present actions. The farmer cannot simply view the land as a producing agency which for his life time will yield up enough to keep him comfortable, if what he does to it renders it progressively less productive. One does have to ask questions other than those concerned with immediate personal benefit. We have to ask the question of what ought to be. That is not a scientific question, but it is a question which is given sharp focus by what modern science has now made possible for man.

A more sinister aspect of this question is that man can destroy himself. A few misunderstood words in an earphone, the pressing of a couple of buttons, the caprice of a dictator or the anger of an outraged gentleman politician and widespread destruction could follow in a matter of minutes. Man has the possibility of destroying within a very short while the very conditions in which human life on the planet are possible.

One does not like to dwell upon such possibilities, but they should not escape our attention. Let us mention a third consideration, that of priorities. In assessing how science will be applied to human interests, someone in authority has to consider what is most important. If getting to the moon and beyond is more important than the conquest of cancer then more considerable efforts will be devoted to the former than to the latter task. This will, of course, be acclaimed by all who stand to benefit from the operation. The average man cannot see beyond the personal security for which he labours for himself and for his family. So his response will be: 'Sure, it's a good project! It provides work for us all, doesn't it?' Here it is not quite the same sort of problem as the conquest of Everest, let's say. For so much more is involved. We might admire the answer to the question 'Why climb Everest?' 'Because it's there!' But that just will not do about the moon. The moon is, of course, there. But the resources necessary to get man to the moon, keep him there, etc. (and going to the moon is a symbol for so much else in the way of space-travel and exploration) the effort and time, and social re-organization of life on earth, were this really to become a priority, makes it a quite different proposition from the conquest of Everest.

We ought not to measure the possible values of proposed achievements simply in narrowly selfish terms, whether personal or national. There are wider considerations.

Our point is that when the question about the future is raised, as it must be raised, in reference to the work of the scientist, and to the application of the scientific know-how, we have to raise *moral issues*. In raising such issues, the scientist is, of course, involved, since he too, is a member of the human community. However, he may not be particularly competent in such matters. The respect which is due to him as scientist should not lead to undue respect for whatever he says.

Summary and Conclusion

Science as applied to human life has made it complex and at times threatening. The question has become pressing in view of man's increasing capacity and knowledge, Who is to exercise the necessary control which will keep life and the world liveable for man? We can no longer think in narrowly selfish terms. Someone must raise the moral issues involved in considering the use to which the powers we have will be put.

Science and the Future

Discussion Questions

Should the scientist be held responsible for the use of the things which he produces? If not, who should?

Should technological production proceed unhindered?

Should the scientist be allowed control over fellow-human beings in the name of scientific progress?

In which ways are we, ordinary citizens, private human beings involved in the future of science and technology?

What is the difference between a scientific and a moral question?

Is the future unpredictable?

12 | Religion and the Future

TAKE the case of the man who invests in a life insurance policy. He starts at forty-three and he goes on until sixty-three. Why? He has a concern about a particular part of the future, and wishes to be secure in several specifiable respects. When it comes near time for retirement he will know that worries which he otherwise might have had have been avoided. If he thinks about the possibility of being involved in an accident, he knows that his family will be more secure than they would otherwise have been without the insurance. He has a particular concern about a limited future.

We can be concerned about the future in different ways. Not every concern about the future is religious. But the interesting fact is that many religions do have a genuine concern about the future. This does not mean that they are simply interested in predicting what will happen. Prediction need not be religious at all. Nor, of course, need it be right! Nevertheless a persisting strand which a student of different religions notices, and cannot help noticing, is that religions have been, and are, concerned about the future. To the question, 'What is the relation between the present and the future?' various religions have responded by talking about goodness and badness for one thing, and about God for another.

As to the first, it is said that the goodness or badness of the present human life has some influence upon the sort of future the believer can expect. Heaven is the goal of the good, and hell is the goal of the bad. There may be a time of purging, getting the residual bad out of man, to prepare the evil ones for a good hereafter. However this sort of idea is expressed (and if you are interested you can follow it up), the important thing to notice is that a *moral* connection is made between the present and the future. Good in the present leads to a good future. Bad in the present leads to a bad future.

But is this a particularly *religious* concern about the future? You can talk about good and bad without being religious, in fact without being moral. You can predict the future without being either religious or moral. In fact, as we have seen, the aim of the scientist is to win control over nature, and this control is measured by his ability to predict. But let us take some down-to-earth examples. If you eat sour apples you will be likely to have an upset stomach. If you keep on inhaling tars from cigarettes you are liable to become prone to lung cancer. If you go to a good driving school and apply what you learn, you will, most likely, have a good safety record. In each of our cases we have co-ordinated what we can call *causes* with *effects*. Given the cause the effect is probable. But in each case, and this includes the scientist as well, the concern with the future is with a limited bit of the world or of history.

We may be concerned with seeing that the future is kept fit for man and his needs. The problem which we discussed relative to science was whether in some way our hope for the future could be secured by some sort of control over what will issue in that future. This is neither a scientific nor a religious concern. A moral concern is not necessarily a religious concern. Nor is every concern for the future a moral one. It may simply be prudential. If I now take out life insurance, then I shall have at some future time a financial security that I should (perhaps) not otherwise have.

Not every concern for the future expressed in the name of religion is a religious concern. For example a programme of political action endorsed by a religious community may not be religious. A programmed apocalyptic time-table may be heartily believed within a religious community, but may not be religious. We must recall our definition of religion as a concern for the ground and goal of human life that is set forth in the light of some understanding of what is wrong with man. The concern about the future that is *religious* will be related to the fundamental question and concern about human existence.

The way to analyse our problem is to take examples from different religions and to see what *kind* of attitude is taken to the future, and how this is expressed. For this purpose we shall consider examples from Islam (the Koran), from Judaism (the Old Testament) and from Christianity (the New Testament).

Read the following: Isaiah 35, Daniel 12:1–3, Malachi 4:1–3,

Revelation 20:11–15, 22:1–6 (see selection at the end of the chapter). The Koran chapters 37, 33, 44, 83 (the relevant passages will be found on the following pages: 166–8, 289–90, 146, 49–50 of the Penguin edition).

The following features are characteristic of the religious concern for the future, as is illustrated from these passages:

1. The future concerns not simply this or that individual but *humanity*, all men. Since the particular religion has its own answer to what the trouble with man is, it diagnoses the *fault* in him in relation to what he might have been or what he ought to be. The future of mankind has to do with the analysis of what the something is that is wrong with him.

2. The future with which religions are concerned is *beyond the present life*. The solution to his problem comes to man from beyond himself, from a trans-historical source.

3. Religious teachings about the future, if not merely moral, *have a very important moral element*. They express the faith that there is a good future for goodness, that is to say the kind of life which is now, in this existence, and has a direct relationship to the kind of future that will be endured or enjoyed. Heaven and hell are persistent ways of expressing this relationship.

4. Convictions about the future are *expressed in picture language*, in what has been called myth. Now picture language can be taken literally, as depicting photographable reality. But that may not be the point of it, and in taking it that way, we may miss the intention of the writer. This is true even if the writer claims that what he writes about he has seen in a vision. This still leaves the question: What is the vision about? The other way of taking the language of vision is to understand it as pointing to a meaning which the author is expressing in a way different from straightforward propositions. We are led into utter absurdity if we really try to take some of the visions as descriptive rather than symbolical. After all how can one express truth about a trans-historical reality except in some form of picture language, some form of symbol? We shall not be put off by the pictures, nor confined by them.

5. For the religious concern, the future *is connected with the idea of God*, his purposes and his activity. In brief, a question about the future is a religious question when it is a question about God. Concern about the future is religious where God is associated with

fulfilment or lack of it. This is true in a limited and in a wider sense. When the prophets looked at the movements of the great powers of their time, Egypt, Assyria, Babylon, Persia, they were convinced that the events which transpired in the wake of these movements were not simply fortuitous, but that they fulfilled the purpose of Yahweh, the God who had made himself known in the history of the Hebrews. History was not haphazard but, even if it appeared to be meaningless and even frightful, it was to be seen as expressing the will of Yahweh. So they could speak of Yahweh's control of the future, immediate or more distant. History was not merely political or military. Yahweh's will was expressed in what had taken place, and would be expressed in what would come. This interpretation of the future was religious in that it was associated in their minds with the transcendent, the ultimate—with God.

This idea of the purpose and activity of a transcendent God expressed in historical events had a wider application. God was associated with the goal of human existence. In a monotheistic religion, faith that God is one, is ultimate and is active, secures the future against meaninglessness. The kind of meaning it gives to the future by associating that future with man's ultimate concern is a religious one.

We have come back to point 1. Religions talk about the future in terms of the fulfilment of human need, the achievement of human destiny.

We have seen that when the scientist deals with the question of the future he must use non-scientific language to express himself. We have seen that in the religious expressions of concern about the future the language of myth is used. The question thus raised is 'Which are the most adequate symbols to use?' The scientist does not have the resources, in his capacity as scientist, to frame such symbols. Religious symbols will inevitably be used to portray man's concern about the future. We must be sure that they are adequate.

When is a religious symbol adequate? The question means, When does a religious symbol, for example heaven, hell, resurrection (since we are talking about the future), perform an essential function for the believer? We are here speaking of *religious* adequacy, and should recall our observations about religion as

Religion and Science

having to do with the fundamental problem that human beings face. If that is at all correct, an adequate religious symbol will have some connection with the raising and answering—not simply on an intellectual level—of that problem. It will have to do with the living of the problem.

There would, it would seem, be at the least two features of a religious symbol if adequate. It is adequate first, when it speaks to the 'depths' in man, serving to focus his hopes, insights and feelings—in short, his experience—and to evoke a response of a proper kind. If the response is the right response the symbol is serving its purpose adequately. A symbol stands for that which is other than itself. A reality is pointed to, portrayed, represented. When the symbol is a living one, it evokes a right response to the reality so pointed to.

Second, a religious symbol is adequate when it cannot be *adequately* translated into non-mythical language, that is to say when there is no substitute for it. The function of symbol is not primarily to convey an idea. This can be achieved by a theological or a philosophical statement. The symbol is thus 'closer' to the experience of the religious person.

Conversely then a symbol is inadequate if it does not speak to the depths in man. Some symbols which once did now no longer evoke responses of a proper kind. Some once powerful symbols have now no longer the power to point. A cultural change brings with it a whole new range of symbols and makes obsolete a range of old symbols. To speak of God as shepherd and as Lord in a feudal and agricultural society would have had much greater impact than it would in an urban and democratic society.

If we defend the use of a symbol it will be because it does what can't be done in any other way. Turning to the symbols that have recurred in this chapter, do the symbols (heaven, hell, resurrection) express 'thoughts' that do lie too deep for words'? Do they express something of fundamental importance with respect to the human problem? Do they answer to human experience?

You can, of course, only answer meaningfully for yourself. But one or two observations might help. Many people have felt that there is an 'order' within the universe, a 'scheme of things', that their grasp of right and wrong is not an illusion but is representative of how things are, that there is going to be a victory for right,

Religion and the Future

and goodness, that human wickedness and natural evil is a blot which will eventually be wiped out. Hence the meaningfulness of 'heaven' and 'hell'. Also there has been a 'feeling' that human life should not end with death, a conviction that it won't. This gives power to the symbol of resurrection.

Such symbols are an invitation not simply to consider the doctrine, but to 'live' the experience which underlies it, and without which it has no real meaning. The symbol focuses the invitation and nurtures the experience when it becomes present.

Addendum: Selection of Statements about the future from Religious Literature

From the Old Testament

The day comes, glowing like a furnace; all the arrogant and the evil doers shall be chaff, and that day when it comes shall set them ablaze, says the LORD of Hosts, it shall leave them neither root nor branch. But for you who fear my name, the sun of righteousness shall rise with healing in his wings, and you shall break loose like calves released from the stall. On the day that I act, you shall trample down the wicked, for they will be ashes under the soles of your feet, says the LORD of Hosts.

Malachi 4:1–3

At that moment Michael shall appear,
   Michael the great captain,
   who stands guard over your fellow-countrymen;
   and there will be a time of distress
   such as has never been
   since they became a nation till that moment.
But at that moment your people will be delivered,
   every one who is written in the book:
Many of those who sleep in the dust of the earth will wake,
   some to everlasting life
   and some to the reproach of eternal abhorrence.
The wise leaders shall shine like the bright vault of heaven,
   and those who have guided the people in the true path
   shall be like the stars for ever and ever.

Daniel 12:1–3

Religion and Science

From the New Testament

Then I saw a new heaven and a new earth, for the first heaven and the first earth had vanished, and there was no longer any sea. I saw the holy city, new Jerusalem, coming down out of heaven from God, made ready like a bride adorned for her husband. I heard a loud voice proclaiming from the throne: 'Now at last God has his dwelling among men! He will dwell among them and they shall be his people, and God himself will be with them. He will wipe every tear from their eyes; there shall be an end to death and to mourning and crying and pain; for the old order has passed away!'

Then he who sat on the throne said, 'Behold! I am making all things new!' (And he said to me, 'Write this down, for these words are trustworthy and true. Indeed they are already fulfilled.') 'I am the Alpha and the Omega, the beginning and the end. A draught from the water-springs of life will be my free gift to the thirsty. All this is the victor's heritage; and I will be his God and he shall be my son. But as for the cowardly, the faithless, and the vile, murderers, fornicators, sorcerers, idolators, and liars of every kind, their lot will be the second death, in the lake that burns with sulphurous flames.'

Revelation 21:1–8

From the Koran

The Day of Judgement is the appointed time for all. On that day no man shall help his friend; none shall be helped save those on whom Allah will have mercy. He is the Mighty One, the Merciful.

The fruit of the Saqqum-tree shall be the sinner's food. Like dregs of oil, like scalding water, it shall simmer in his belly. A voice will cry: 'Seize him and drag him into the depth of Hell. Then pour boiling water over his head, saying: "Taste this, illustrious and honourable man! This is the punishment which you doubted."'

As for the righteous, they shall dwell in peace together amidst gardens and fountains, arrayed in rich silks and fine brocade. Yes, and we shall wed them to dark-eyed houris. Secure against all ills, they shall call for every kind of fruit; and having died once, they shall die no more. Your Lord will through His mercy shield them from the scourge of Hell. That will be the supreme triumph.

Chapter 44: Smoke

As for the true servants of Allah, a generous provision shall be made for them; they shall feast on fruit and be honoured in the gardens of delight. Reclining face to face upon soft couches they shall be served with a goblet filled at a gushing fountain. Their drink shall neither dull their senses nor befuddle them. And by their side shall sit bashful, dark-eyed virgins, as chaste as the sheltered eggs of ostriches....

Is this not a better welcome than the Zaqqum tree? We have made this tree a scourge for the wrongdoers. It grows in the nethermost part of Hell, bearing fruit like devil's heads: on it they shall feed, and with it they shall cram their bellies, together with draughts of scalding water. Then to Hell they shall return.

Chapter 37: The Ranks

Summary and Conclusion

A religious concern for the future has to do with the fundamental question about human existence. It is different from other kinds of concern in that it has to do with humanity, that it looks beyond the present life, has a strong moral element, is expressed in symbols and talks about God. The symbols are adequate if they evoke an adequate response and if they perform a function that cannot be performed otherwise.

Discussion Questions

Why do you think that heaven and hell feature so regularly in religious thought?

Find and discuss symbols used to interpret the future.

What is the future?

Man is essentially a creature of hope. Take hope from him and he ceases to be human. Yet he knows he ought to do good. Discuss.

Do you think that death interrupts the future? Is there a religious attitude to death?

13 | *The Question about Beginnings*

IN THE previous chapter we made a distinction between prudential, moral and religious concern. We can now spell out this distinction in a little greater detail.

A religious concern takes place on a different level, at a different depth of the human person than the others and has to do with, not simply a bit of this life, but with the very meaning and fulfilment of life itself. So it tries to pierce beyond the merely secular and temporal concerns to the origin, ground, end and fulfilment of human being itself. As it does so it uses language in what seems, in contrast to the secular usage of such language, to be a very strange way. So, in regard to the future the believer talks not simply about life, but about 'eternal' life, the adjective serving to qualify the ordinary term, and so pointing us to look and demanding us to think in an appropriate way. Concern about 'eternal' life is on a different level from concern about life (the life in the expression 'life insurance' for example). The term 'eternal' refers to an ultimate level of reality and of concern.

Religion can, then, be seen as a particular kind of concern. Whatever that concern is *about*, whatever comes within the orbit of that concern is of religious interest. We have seen how this has worked out in reference to the future. Now let us have a look at how it might work out in reference to the past. As to the future, the believer says that God (or the gods) is (or are) in life-giving relationship with man, which it is hoped extends *beyond* the present and individual existence. If it can be thought of as extending forward into the future, it can also be thought of as extending backward (so to speak).

Let us pause here to observe that we do ask questions about where we have come from, why we are here and where we are going. Such questions can be asked on the life-insurance level.

The Question about Beginnings

But, even though we may not press it, we may have a niggling feeling that there are other ways of asking the question, and that there are other kinds of answer beside the life-insurance kind of answer. Now, since other kinds of answer than the life-insurance kind of answer have been proposed to the basic questions we have raised, we must realize that if we want to understand the answer we have to feel the problem. It may be just as important, sometimes more important, to ask the right questions as to hear the answers. It would seem that two conditions must be present for understanding to follow: 1, we must inquire in the proper way; 2, we must have a spirit of inquiry.

There are some kinds of inquiry which can only be successful when the person asking the question is involved in the answers that are suggested, and is involved in such a way that he is restless until some kind of satisfaction is achieved. When we've really got a question, we've also got an interest and an incentive. The answer becomes important. Ultimate questions are always relevant because they ask about human beings. These persisting questions are the concern of religion, which relates man to some power and destiny and origin beyond himself, in order to answer the fundamental question about himself.

Remember an important rule: Don't dismiss the answer until you understand the question.

This same question means something different when it is a religious question from what it does when it is an historical or a scientific question. We can see that the question in different from the different kinds of answer that we get. Since we get different answers, this means that the question is a different one when asked by different people. Let us sample some answers we get to it.

The scientist addresses himself to the question, 'How did the universe get going?' He gathers all the data about galaxies and pulsars and quasars, stars and planets and then frames a theory as to how they may have come to be what they are now, and then how they came to be. So it may be in terms of a 'big bang' (or many big bangs), or in terms of a steady state. Having suggested how the data might be interpreted *qua* theoretical astronomer he has no further suggestions to make.

The historian takes the question to mean, 'How did human

culture get going?' Making a distinction between pre-history and history, the former beyond the range of his interest because it is beyond the range of his evidence, he musters the evidence he has and suggests how it was when man first left behind traces that could yield information adequate enough to re-construct what his life and relations were like. He can only go back a limited way. Ask him *how* things began and he gives his own kind of answer, which is descriptive as far as he can make it. That means, as far as he feels confident in interpreting the evidence which he has. He answers an historian's question, using the appropriate ways of inquiry. Note here that some of the historical evidence may be obtained only by the scientist, that certain sciences are concerned with the history of the earth.

The question about beginnings for the religious believer, or inquirer, is posed on a different level. What he means by it is: How is it that there is anything when there might have been nothing? Notice that the form of the question has changed. It is now a 'how is it that' question rather than 'how' question. 'How is it that' means 'Why?' The kind of answer that he gives (different believers giving different variations of it) is this one: God created the whole lot. A religious concern about origins, like a religious concern about the future, talks about God (or the gods, or some equivalent), relates that talk to *human* problems (every religion suggesting that there is something wrong with human being), talks in terms of a beyond-ordinary-existence, using symbols to express itself.

Some symbols are put together in a narrative form. These we call myths. A myth provides a unifying framework for the symbols used in the form of a narrative.

Note that the term 'myth' has two adjectives, 'mythical' and 'mythological'. The former means 'not historically or scientifically true', the latter is neutral as to factuality. We are using 'myth' in this neutral sense.

For the philosopher and the theologian a conceptual scheme rather than a myth provides the framework for his symbols. But myth is closer to the concrete reality of the religious concern than the conceptual scheme. The myth may later get translated into the conceptual scheme. This will not mean that concept is 'better'. The functions are different. The myth employs a narrative form. It is a story. Not any sort of story, but the kind of story about which you ought to ask, 'What is its meaning?' You may get quite off the track if instead of asking 'What is its meaning?' you insist on asking 'Did it really happen this way?' (Which way?) A myth is a myth because it is not to be taken as narrative *au pied de la lettre*. If your answer to that is that that is not your problem, then mine is 'If that is not a problem, it is not a problem'. But for some people it is a very great problem.

But assuming that we may move on from that problem, we notice that there are persistent myths which have been told in the great religions of the world which purport to take us back in time to beginnings, not simply this or that beginning but to the beginning of everything. Now that is the odd thing to do. After all why not simply be content with the explanation of effects with causes, assuming the order of the universe as we know it? Why worry about such strange questions about the 'first cause' 'first mover' of the whole thing? Indeed since we only know causes by observing effects, it would not seem that we *could* justifiably and meaningfully go beyond the causal catena and speak about a cause beyond that. There seems to be a dilemma. If we speak of God as first cause we bring him within the range of scientific explanation, and here we draw a blank. If we claim that God is cause but other than the sort of cause we know, then we seem to be talking nonsense.

Religions have persisted with the story of God who created the earth. Our questions, 'Why did things begin?' 'Why is there something when there might have been nothing?' must be understood by the answer given to them. We understand the question by the answer.

What sort of an answer is 'God created all things' then? The believer expresses his faith that human life has meaning, to be found by reference to a reality other than and greater than himself, that what is wrong with human life can be healed in relation to this reality and to this purpose. If this conviction is expressed in temporal terms, it will come out in the language of past and future, for both of which symbols and myths will be used. If that which transcends human life gives purpose and healing to human life, and if it (he, He) is genuinely ultimate, then it can be no accident, nor can it have just happened. If it (he, He) has cosmic significance then the whole works depends upon Him (taking the Christian and Hebrew version), and if that is so it is not just now but for ever—or as long as in the past there has been human life. The teaching about creation expresses man's final and utter dependence upon God, however you thereafter go on to explain how it was that human life came to be. That is for another level of explanation. A rightly understood religious teaching about creation, origins, does not get into conflict with the other kinds of answer to the question about origins, providing that those answers recognize their limitations too. However God created, *that* He created means that everything that is came to be as a result of His will and purpose. This (and more) is what is meant by the most puzzling confession that speaks of *creatio ex nihilo*. If everything has its ground in God, everything will find its fulfilment in God. The religious answer is quite specific. Its understanding of the answer gives a specific kind of meaning to the question which we are asking.

This expression *creation out of nothing* is well worth considering further. It is, remember, an answer given to a question. The question to which it is proposed as an answer is not the kind of question about *how* things operate, given things operating. It is not the sort of answer which attempts to co-ordinate empirically discernible fact with empirically discernible fact, to find order in the relations between them. It is not *that* sort of concept. It could not serve as a basis of scientific prediction or assist in the expression in mathematical terms of the data to which it refers. It does not help to relate some 'second causes' with other 'second causes'. It is on a different level of claim than that. It goes beyond how the order operates to say something about the whole order of things itself. In that it goes beyond the physical order, it is a *metaphysical* statement.

It helps in looking at theological statements to see what they exclude. For what they do not say, and what they say ought not to be said may be as important as what they do say. Indeed such theological statements prescribe limits within which we are invited to operate. What then of the statement 'God created the world out of nothing'?

First, it intends to deny that the world is part of God. Pantheism, the view that God is all and all is God, is quite clearly here denied. The world is not God. It was created out of nothing, not out of God. It has an independence of God. It is an order in its own right. What happens within it is not direct divine causation. There is an order of 'second causes'. Such a view is congenial ground for the investigation of the realm of 'second', independent causes. It provided the milieu for the rise of modern science in the West. The Christian need have no divided mind about investigating *how* this independent world operates.

Second, and this will seem to be somewhat contradictory, but it will turn out to be a paradox rather than a contradiction, *Creatio ex nihilo* denies that ultimately the world is self-explanatory, and ultimately independent. Thus it affirms the dependence of the world upon God. *Creation* is the language of action. God created. Thus what is created is an expression of will and of purpose. It is thus the will of God that the world be both dependent on and independent of him. Whatever his purpose shall be, it will be manifest within the creation (here = 'the created order of things') which he has brought about, but which has a relative independence of him.

Notice that a scientific attitude would not be inclined to deny either of these meanings. As to the first, the scientist would, if he thought about it, affirm the settled order of the world with which his concepts operate, whether or not he thought any further about the significance of there being such an order. But that measure of agreement with the theist is significant and sufficient as a basis for further discussion, in which one could seek to explore further what the significance was.

In the second case we would have to move beyond scientific grounds to affirm the ultimate dependence or purposefulness of the world, especially if we did not identify the world and God as we are forbidden to do by the *creatio ex nihilo* formula. That is to say, there is no scientific basis for denying or affirming that the world is purposive, that it is good. That is a metaphysical statement and so is its denial. If we see a pattern in the world (see last chapter of the book) it will not be because we are good scientists. It will be because we see and experience and interpret things in a certain way.

Summary and Conclusion

The religious question about beginnings extends beyond the present and individual existence. The scientists and historian ask, 'How did things begin?' The religious question is 'How is it that (=Why) did things begin?' Symbols are used in giving the answer. A series of symbols put together in narrative form is called a myth. The statement that God created all things, especially if one adds 'out of nothing', denies that God and the world are identical and affirms the relative independence of the world. It also, paradoxically, claims that the world is dependent upon God. The scientist will not be inclined *qua* scientist to deny either of these claims.

Discussion Questions

Read Genesis chapters one and two. What sort of account do you think these provide? Is there any kind of scientific theory which such an account would contradict? Could either a steady state theory or a big bang theory be harmonized with it? If so, how?

Why do religions employ myth? Collect some creation myths and interpret them in non-mythical terms. Do you find any common themes in the emerging versions?

14 | Revelation

'TO REVEAL' means to make known what was not before known. It carries also the idea that what is known comes to be known because of an activity on the part of the revealer. So the word is different in significance from 'discovery', where the activity is on the part of the one who comes to know. I discover something. I have something revealed to me. If you will think about some of the ways we use the word in common parlance you will discover that it has this two-fold significance.

Take the following examples: The curtain was drawn and the plaque was revealed. She removed the veil and revealed her face. Actress reveals all. A slip of the tongue revealed his true intentions. A grimace revealed that he was in pain. The X-ray pictures revealed that he was free of disease. We may now reveal who the donor was.

In each of these seven cases certain interesting features are clear. When the curtain or the veil is drawn aside, something that was not known before now comes to be known. That is of the essence of the meaning of revelation. What was once unknown is now known. The revealing act is often intentional. There are some things I can never know unless the act of another person makes them available to me. Sometimes the knowledge then has to do with the person doing the revealing sometimes not. The 'all' which the actress reveals may be herself. It may not! She may be revealing who the train robbers were.

Sometimes there is a medium, an intermediary through which the new knowledge is made possible. You have to consider the significance of the grimace (Is the man a comedian?) and of the X-ray pictures (Are they really good photographs?). And who is to say whether my interpretation of the 'slip of the tongue' when it's different from yours is the right interpretation? If I'm going

Religion and Science

to get you to see the validity of *my* interpretation I'm going to have to present reasons to you, to discuss the matter wiht you and try to convince you of the reasonableness of my interpretation.

Religions talk about God and about revelation. They claim to have had revealed to them some knowledge of God. The claim to revelation in different religions focuses upon different stretches of history and is linked with different people. If God is x, it is then a question of defining x in some way or other. The different religions, among other things, define or speak of God and his activity in particular ways. The basic claim of a religion is that God has become known. He is now known whereas before the coming into being of that religion, he was not known, as he now is. So we are invited to look at a little or a large piece of history, at one event or a series of events that are interpreted as providing the clue to the meaning of x.

So many things have happened in the course of human life upon the earth that it is bewildering to behold the mosaic, let alone to find some evidence of purpose within it. People do things; groups relate to groups; great individuals arise; life changes and goes on changing. Is it possible that in the midst of the welter of the unpredictable change some really decisive meaning can be found? Within the Judaeo-Christian tradition, it is not only claimed that there can, but that certain events give content to x. So, it is said, God is revealed at the Exodus. God is revealed in the Cross.

When religion claims that God, be he Yahweh, or the Father, or Allah, has revealed himself, there goes along with *that* claim the other one that something decisive has happened bearing upon *human* beings. It would indeed be most difficult to know what could be meant by a revelation of God that had nothing to do with the human condition.

Theology is the attempt to understand the revelation of God, or the claim that he has revealed himself. Theological understanding is inevitable in the religious community. Every believer has a theology. He has no choice. It will either be a good one or a bad one. Those people who make it their task to understand and to present that understanding to others as a profession are called theologians. They attempt to clarify, by relating and explaining the different implications of basic religious experience. Christian

Revelation

theology is based upon the religious experience of the Christian kind.

We may note a parallel between scientific 'experience' and scientific explanation, within the community of science; and religious 'experience' and theological explanation, within the believing community. Interpretation and experience are interwoven for the experience to be understood. Indeed, we have seen that for the scientist (and the historian), there can be no data without interpretation. So it is with the theologian. There is knowledge where the conditions of receptivity have been met. We have seen already that testability or appeal to public confirmation means availability to the right people in the right circumstances with the right abilities. It is true both in religion and in science that not everyone is able to understand what is being said. It appears to them as nonsense, as we have seen.

This does not mean that you have to be a scientist or a believer for much of what is said and written to make sense. For religion may be taken on two levels: 1, as a phenomenon to be dealt with along with other phenomena. Sacred books will then be understood as records of those who have claimed to have participated in the phenomenon, whose perspectives can be understood as an account of human experiences and understandings. Lines of development can be traced. Concepts can be compared. Contrasts and comparisons can be made with other religions, and with concepts and understandings drawn from non-religious understandings and experience; 2, As something participated in. In this case the experiences recorded in, let us say, the Bible are seen as continuous with one's own, within the presently existing community. The Biblical accounts are not simply reports of interesting but distant phenomena. They are rather the means for a present revealing of the God of whom they speak. You are, so to speak, part of the experiment, involved with the exercise, instead of reading of it, in a report. You are doing the research, not simply reading about it at a distance. The involvement, which can be compared in at least some respects with the involvement of the scientist, is what makes the difference.

The work of the scientist is done within the scientific community, which is well-defined. It has its rules and norms. Its body of opinion and process of assessment is well-established and universally operative. It is the milieu for research and discovery and for the humdrum pedantry of the working scientist. It is a brave man who goes against the opinion of the establishment in the various branches of science. When revolutions occur in scientific thinking and procedure and theory it is because a long long process of attrition has already taken place and there is no alternative. The community provides the incentives, through its conferences, its journals, its commendations for the worthy and had its way of ignoring or censuring or criticizing the unworthy. The scientific community is an historical reality with its values, ethics, and shared experience. There are normative periods (of discovery rather than revelation) to which it can look: to the century of genius and to Newton; to the phenomenon of Einstein, for example, in the history of physics. (It would be most interesting, but not appropriate at this point, to set out in detail the ways in which the scientist is related to his past in comparison and contrast with the ways in which the theologian is related to his past.)

In each case we are dependent upon the presence of participating community for there to be anything to understand upon level 1. We shall find available to us a bewildering variety of interpretations of religion. Even within the context of Christian faith, understanding will require openness, some industry, willingness to suspend judgement. For some people, it will involve becoming participant in the experiment and venture.

We now look at certain fundamental Christian claims with the above distinction in mind. In any particular theology these *basic* claims will be expressed differently. There will be different emphases. There will also be different conceptual structures and ideas. Part of the task of a living theology is to talk about the convictions of the faith in concepts that have currency at any particular period. We suggest the following as basic claims:

What Jesus Christ said, what he did and what happened to him provide the proper foundation for Christian faith, and its understanding of God.

Jesus Christ reveals God, the problem of man, and the solution to that problem.

God was active in the history of Jesus Christ, both before and after his death. This includes the continuing reality of the Christian community. It also makes central an understanding of the Resurrection.

Such claims are faith-claims. They are to be preceded by the confession 'I (or we) believe'.

Having stated certain fundamental Christian claims, let us now connect them with the idea of revelation.

We can take as the fundamental claim, the claim that gives status to all other claims, that *revelation has taken place*. Reasonable content has been given to the term 'God' through the experience and issues in propositional claims, for example that God is love. It does not in its essence consist in the communication of propositions, but in the creation of a level of being, the heightening of awareness, the deepening of conviction, the assurance of presence, and of meaning. This is then expressed in propositions.

The Christian says such things in relation to Jesus. But how are we to understand how or why he connects such present revelation with events which have long since happened? How can the Christian reasonably speak about awareness, conviction, presence, meaning in relation to Jesus, a figure from the past, in today's world? We said above that the Christian seeks to give a reasonable content to the term 'God'. This means that we can discuss it, give reasons for it, try to explain it.

What can it mean to say that something is revealed in a stretch of history, continuous with the one in which we now live? We may draw a parallel to our national history. An Englishman participating in the institutions of a particular society insists that his children be taught English history. England is the place where English history is taught. In America, the American boy will know very little of it. But he should know quite a bit about American history. In Austria, the school children learn Austrian history. The Italian will learn Italian history. Now the English history which the American does learn, and the Austrian history which the Italian learns will be both selective and biased (using the term in an unbiased sense). We are our history. Our history has made us what we are. The value we know, the very sharing of the community (or communities) in which we live is tied to history (or histories). Different histories make different people(s). There have come to us, from beyond us in time, traditions which to influence us consciously must be learned. But they influence us whether we learn of them or not. They are an objective reality coming to us from the past, shaping our knowledge, our attitudes and our morals.

So with the revelation claimed within the Christian history. There has come, through the centuries, a set of beliefs, of values, a kind of community which has its fundamental grounding and origin in a stretch of history: the history of Jesus Christ. Theological understanding thus rests upon two primary foundations: the fact of the history of Jesus Christ and the fact of the continuing community of worship.

There is also what we might call the size of the claim which the believer is making for his faith. For him revelation has to do with the ultimate, with the whole. This makes his claim to be a very far-reaching one and so an important one, whether it is right or not.

Summary and Conclusion

Revelation is the coming to know what was not known before. It creates a community of believers and is expressed in the confessions of faith which represent a reality in the present which has been shaped by past events taken to be of crucial importance.

Discussion Questions

Make a list of sentences with the word 'reveal', or 'revelation' in them. Proceed then to frame a definition of the word based on observations about the usage. Is the religious use of the word basically different from its common usage?

How is it possible to say that a series of events in the past reveals God? For example the life, teachings, death and resurrection of Jesus Christ?

Why do theologians disagree?

15 | Faith

WE OBSERVED at the end of the previous chapter that the claims of the religious person are prefaced with the words 'I believe' or some equivalent to this. The primary claim is, 'I believe in God'. These statements are, as we say, 'confessions of faith'. What does it mean to say 'I believe'? This way of speaking is not, of course unique to the believer. Does he then believe in a special way? Since the words 'believe', 'belief' are used in different senses, a job of sorting out needs to be done to clarify what the religious use of the term is actually claiming. Such a procedure will prove illuminating.

Let us start with four sentences whose meaning we quite well understand.

I. I believe that it's half past two.
II. I believe in penicillin.
III. I believe in Chelsea.
IV. I believe in you.

Note now that while there are two nouns *belief* and *faith*, there is only one single verb corresponding to each of these. This is the verb to believe. So while we talk of believing, we do not speak of faithing. Because of this the word 'to believe' may mean to have belief, or it may mean to have faith. We must make up our minds in any particular case. We must be careful to distinguish the uses of the word, so that its various meanings do not get confused. For if they do, then the proper meaning of faith is bound to be obscured. By 'proper' we mean the appropriate meaning in the particular context. If we have alternatives in mind, we may better decide in any given context which is the appropriate meaning of the term. We shall then not simply transfer one meaning to each case, or one inadequate meaning to the particular context. For example, 'believing' might mean 'accepting as true on inadequate evidence'. Whether that is an adequate meaning will depend upon the usage to which it is put. If the context demands that usage, then the meaning it has is a proper one. But this does not mean that 'believe' will always have this meaning.

Going then to our examples:

In the first instance, 'I believe' means 'I am of the opinion that', 'I am more or less certain that' what I am saying is correct. What is being affirmed is *the correctness (more or less) of a fact*. You could easily give other examples: I believe you can get to New York from London in five hours; I believe that Mary is Jane's cousin; I believe that Sarah Jones is a pen-name for Susan Jenkins, etc.

In the case of II and III, the term 'I believe in' expresses the confidence appropriate to what is believed in. 'I believe in penicillin' means that you would recommend its use, you would use it yourself, because it would produce benefit when used. 'I believe in Chelsea' (a football team, of course) means that you think that they are likely to have success rather than failure. In both of these cases the confidence expressed is tested by future performance. If penicillin produced such dreadful side-effects that outweighed its future usefulness you would not talk this way about it. If Chelsea never won a game for the whole of the season you would soon lose that confidence. 'I believe in' in the sense *I have confidence in* is a statement which you can alter if you find that things don't turn out so as to bear out your confidence. You have to wait and see!

We may not be aware of the total range of our confidence. We assume beliefs, which we only make explicit when there is some demand upon us or when they are called into question, or when perhaps, for methodological purposes, we feel that examination is called for to make them explicit. The physical scientist has a confidence of this kind. He assumes, that is to say he believes in, the reliability of nature, accepting the principle of uniformity as the foundation for all his work. Such an assumption is irrational in the sense that he is never able to give decisive and finally convincing reasons that this is so. But his whole activity is based upon this belief being a worthy one. That belief is a non-scientific assumption which, when made, he finds makes his scientific work possible. He

Faith

too has 'faith'. That his methods 'work' is sufficient to sustain that faith.

In the case of IV, we have an example of an expression of personal trust. 'I believe in you', spoken by a father to his son, by a voter to his representative, by a friend to his friend, means 'I trust you'. The term is now being used on a personal level. Of course, it might turn out that such trust is wrongly placed. If you have confidence in a friend and speak to him about private matters and find that the secret is kept your confidence is maintained. But can you be absolutely sure? What if the next time you share a confidence you find that someone later knows about it? Or what if one day you find a knife in your back? But people do trust one another. They do act as if there is not going to be this let-down. They are willing to venture on the assumption that the future will bear out their trust. But they also know that there are quite specific ways in which such trust could be shown to be wrong. But they do not expect that it will. In this fourth sense, then, 'I believe' means *I have trust of a personal kind*.

We will now give our attention to a modern parable.

It is war-time. An enemy has occupied the country. But he does not have it all his own way. For there is an underground resistance movement which is dedicated to thwarting the enemy's plans as far as it is possible. One evening a stranger turns up in the town and makes contact with the resistance people. He spends the whole night in conversation with one of its local leaders, with the result that the stranger convinces him that he is on their side against the enemy. He asks for confidence, whatever the appearances. Then he leaves. But there are others in the underground who are not quite so sure. So when A says, 'We can trust him', B and C say, 'We cannot be so sure'. Sometimes the stranger is the cause of obvious help: a bridge is blown up, and ammunition is sent to the resistance fighters. At other times the picture is not so happy. Hostages are taken and shot. More enemy soldiers are sent to the town. Innocent people are interrogated and tortured. But A goes on saying, 'I believe in the stranger'. B and C say: 'How can you explain the hostages, the soldiers and the torture?' A replies: 'Well, *even though* there is evidence that might seem to point in that direction, *after all* there is other evidence too!' B and C rejoin: 'Yes, but, *even though* there is the bridge blown up, and the supplies, *after all* there are those other things.'

How would you settle an argument like that?

You see, both of them are dealing with the *same facts*. None has any special advantage in knowing about the activities of the stranger what the other does not. They put the whole lot of facts together, some which count for, and some which count against. Then they both say: 'Well, even though' and 'after all'. But they say it in different ways. They find the clue to their attiude by giving different weight to different aspects of the matter.

Does it help if we say, 'Let's wait and see!' When the war is over and we discover that the Germans shoot, or have shot the stranger, or if the British decorate him for his services, would that settle the matter one way or the other?

A would say, and strongly too, that he did not need to wait. He had some basis of assurance which the others did not have. He had had the encounter with the stranger and the conversation through the night, and had then made up his mind. If he were a responsible person, a good judge of character, with experience in intelligence and with a wide acquaintance with resistance agents, his word, his evaluation would be accepted as evidence, even in face of contradictory reports from other people. His 'After all' and 'Well, even though' would be authoritatively spoken. But it could not be taken absolutely. But while he knows that there would be decisive evidence against his faith in the stranger, he does not expect it. So, he knows that he could be shown to be wrong, but he does not expect that he will. That is the strength of his faith. His faith is also a venture.

It seems obvious that all this has something to do with religion. What? Ask, 'Why do some people believe and some people disbelieve?' Both live in the same world. There is suffering, often needless and unproductive suffering; the best efforts of good men for the happiness and security of their fellows are often simply failures; death ends the maturity which it has taken a lifetime to develop; and a great question mark stands over any thought of future existence. That is one side of it.

There is so much beauty too; there is the dream and the vigour of youth dedicated to the dream; there is the giving up of the self and even the life for the sake of noble causes; there is the deter-

Faith

mination to conquer disease, and to build a new world for the future.

The believer is able to point to the tokens of good and say, 'After all there is the good'. The unbeliever says, 'After all there is the suffering'. The believer says, 'Even though there is suffering, there is also the good'. The unbeliever says, 'Even though there is the good there is also the suffering'. But the question is not really settled in that way, any more than there is a basis of argument ultimately between A and his friends B and C in the parable. It was the encounter with the stranger that made the difference for A.

The religious believer claims something along the same lines. It is not for him a matter of having coolly sat down and reasoned the thing out, weighing the probabilities for belief and unbelief carefully and balancing them one against the other. He believes that God has made himself known, and can be trusted. There has been something like an encounter.

This does not mean that he never questions, or doubts. Of course he is sometimes troubled. Of course the shooting of hostages counts against the stranger. He is able to say, 'Well, even though hostages are shot, I can trust him' only after giving the matter careful consideration. His trust is not irrational. It cannot be proved, but it is not irrational. The religious believer has similar questions. There is the unbeliever in every believer, as there is the believer in every unbeliever. We do not believe absolutely. Nor do we disbelieve absolutely. We believe in spite of the appearances. We disbelieve in spite of the appearances. This is because our belief or our unbelief, our faith or lack of faith does not rest upon appearances. We are not argued into faith, and we cannot be argued out of it. Nevertheless it is reasonable. That is the claim of the believer. He will not try to prove it to you, this faith of his. But he will try to show you that it is reasonable. He may even try to persuade you to see things from his perspective. If he does try, he will point to some things as significant and invite you to see the pattern in the whole which he has seen.

Summary and Conclusion

While there are many uses of the term 'I believe' the one most

Religion and Science

appropriate when considering the religious attitude is equivalent to 'I trust'. The believer trusts in God in the same world as the believer who does not. They see the same things but assess them differently. The believer tries to convince the unbeliever that his faith is reasonable. This he does by pointing to what he sees in the world as the clue to the significance of the world as a whole.

Discussion Questions

Can you think of examples of unreasonable faith, trust?

When would you consider it right and proper to stop having confidence in a person whom you trusted?

When would you think it right and proper to put confidence in someone whom you had not trusted?

Why do you think that the Christian religion has spoken of God in terms of personal relations (for example, he is called Father, Judge, King, Comforter)?

Do you have to be certain before you have faith (in)? If not, is faith a matter of greater probability and less? If not, what is the basis of religious faith?

Do you think that there is a sense in which it is right to say that the unbeliever believes, and that the believer lacks faith?

16 | The Pattern of the World

IN EARLIER chapters (5, 15) we took some examples of disagreement about facts. There we raised an interesting problem, namely how if two people both know the same facts and disagree about them, we would settle the dispute.

We also noticed that this is another kind of dispute from a dispute over what the facts are. It is not a matter that could be settled by one party appealing to a fact or facts which the other did not have. In this case it is a question about the right interpretation of the facts that are known to both of them. Such disagreement might take place over relatively simple matters: Is that stuff edible? Is Mary beautiful? Do I deserve a rise? It can get more and more involved, since we are concerned now not with establishing facts but with valuing them. For example: Did John act wisely? Was Mr Brown's conduct of the matter good? Is euthanasia right?

Let us notice that these are examples of a different kind of question from those which science asks. All of these involve the making of value judgements. Of course the scientist is interested in finding pattern in the world. But his interest in such pattern is specialized. The task of any particular scientific discipline is to find and to expound order within the limited context of that discipline's special interests. The scientist cannot rest satisfied until he has brought such order into or evoked it out of nature or history. A scientific fact, as we have seen, is only evident within a framework of scientific theory. Behind such theory is the belief—a working belief—that nature is orderly, that is to say, that it is amenable to the methods of the scientist as he seeks for a certain pattern within it. The scientist, in his capacity as a scientist, working on a part of the whole that there is, does not seek for an overall order, a pattern of the totality. The scientist achieves his purpose when he displays an order within the limited sphere of his interest—an interest which may be very narrow indeed—and in conformity with the appropriate methodology he employs. The larger question about the pattern of the world remains, whatever parallels we may find between the narrower and the broader quest for meaning and for unity. We may or we may not press that larger question, the one that has to do with *all* the facts that we know and with *all* the experiences we have had.

The problem we shall now explore further has to do with the making of a right and proper judgement when we already have all the facts we are going to get. If all the facts are known in a particular case, how does one go about assuring oneself that, when there is disagreement and argument about the perspective, one's interpretation is viable?

In what follows we shall be speaking about the world. By 'world' we mean the totality, the whole, the cosmos, the universe. It stands for what we are able to experience, and can be pointed to in different ways. We could speak of the object, or the subject-matter, the data (or datum) of our experience. 'World' means what is given to us in the totality of our experience, the totality of what impinges upon us and makes experience of many different kinds possible.

We shall have access to the same data within the world. Indeed we may say that the world is our datum. Within this complex of facts that make up our world how shall we take a perspective? When we have done so, how can we know that it is correct or worthy? If we wished to, how could we communicate it?

We do take up such fundamental attitudes. They are not unreasonable, but we may not have been reasoned into them by a process of argument. That means that we shall not be likely to be argued out of them either.

To make our point that the same facts—in this case the death of a village (or large part thereof)—are evaluated differently, remember the following incidents.

While the inhabitants were going about their ordinary activities a volcano erupted and poured its lava over the inhabitants of the village. Death came swiftly and effectively. That is the story of Pompeii.

While the inhabitants slept, the flood swept down from the dam above their village and carried them to their death. That is the story of Longarone.

While the children were finishing their morning prayers the great heap of refuse began to move and engulfed them, with no possibility of escaping from death. That is the story of Aberfan.

The soldiers entered the village with their machine-guns and when they left there was no life left—even the dogs had been shot. That is the story of Lidice.

In these instances we have what we might consider the same fact—the death of a village or large part thereof—within different contexts of human and natural agency. The same fact—x number of people dying—is evaluated differently in the different cases. Indeed in the case of Lidice certain judgements about the proposed act (reprisals following an assassination are right—it is good that these people learn a lesson) led to its being initiated.

In each case we have the same fact, the death of a number of people. We would properly use the term 'tragedy' of each of these dreadful incidents. Yet we would evaluate them differently. In some cases we feel that there is a bigger problem than in others when we try to answer the question 'Why?'

Since there is a sort of inevitability and unpredictability about the operations of nature, since we do not think of nature as having a will of its own, we do not blame 'nature' for natural disasters. We consider the outcome unfortunate when human life is involved, since we consider the preservation of human life to be an obligation, deeming human life to be good. But it does not make sense to speak of nature as having an obligation to preserve human life. In such a natural calamity as at Pompeii the most we can hope is that death came swiftly without pain.

When there is human control of natural processes and things go wrong we are sometimes in something of a quandary. When a dam breaks and the flood waters bring death and devastation we feel that we may blame the builders only if they had not taken enough care and thought. So we mount an enquiry to find out whether this was the case or not. Then we can portion blame and responsibility.

In the Aberfan case, we seek to discover whether there was cause for blame and for concern, whether someone responsible should have acted differently.

In the case of Lidice we feel nothing but outrage. Death caused by human perverseness, and effected in cold blood evokes revulsion, since we feel that nothing can ever justify such malicious and ruthless acts of human will. For, in this case the origin of the death is in the human decision.

Death comes by accident of nature where no human will is involved; death comes where insufficient effort is taken, due perhaps to failure of some human will; death is caused by the deliberate act of human wills. These are not the same deaths. We know why.

We select death as a problem because we all, at some time, feel it as such, whether it is our own or death of others.

We could have made the point in other ways.

Behind the questions and judgements we produce about what happens within the world, there is the question about the sort of world in which such things happen. So there is a big question mark. Is this the sort of world in which one can now discern fulfilment of purpose, or hope for it in the future? We know what happens in our world. What shall we say about it? Is it a good world or isn't it? Is it going to be good or isn't it? Is good going to come out of it or isn't it?

One says, It is an irrational universe, in the end. Granted the order and predictability of the natural processes, when it comes to the question of moral purpose there is no such order and predictability discernible. We are, so to speak, cast adrift in an ocean of forces ultimately unknown and unknowable and cannot discern where we shall be landed, if at all.

Another sees the universe as the scene of a great and endless struggle between good and evil, right and wrong, light and darkness. Now the light seems to be dominant and now the darkness. The alternation is eternal and ultimately unalterable.

The theistic believer claims that the world is rational and purposeful, *however it may now appear*. This does not mean at all that he only looks at what he wishes to see, turning a blind eye to the uncomfortable facts he finds within the world. The intelligent believer who claims that God is creator has real problems to face: about natural disaster, about tragedy caused by human wills, about the fact of death. For if, as he claims, the world and what happens in it manifests a good purpose, such things stand against that purpose.

There are many kinds of fact within our world. We can look at and experience them piecemeal, so to speak, not attempting to put them all together and not asking the big question about them all put together: What does it all mean?

Within the world of our experience there is a multitude of data, which are problematic when you make the attempt to co-ordinate them and try to take up a fundamental attitude to the whole. Not the least of such problems is the problem of pain, suffering and death. It is because there is also so much which we enjoy and which maintains, nurtures and promotes human life and its enjoyment—which we consider to be good—that stands in contrast with pain and death that the problem is so acute. Given both the good (human life and what promotes it) and the bad (the opposite of good) how can we decide about the world in which both are present whether it is good or bad?

When the datum we consider is 'world', the totality rather than a set of facts within the world, we cannot make comparisons. All we have is internal evidence and we are ourselves part of the data. We are not able to make comparisons between this set of facts and another similar or dissimilar set of facts since, by definition, 'world' means everything that is. We must take up a stance within this set of facts or not at all. Not to take a stance, i.e. to say 'we cannot know', is itself a stance. It is called agnosticism. So we do not escape taking a stance even if we do not want to take one, or to be explicit about it. While the data are 'all things that there are' there are no more than that. If we make a decision we have to make it on the basis of what we experience and know of the world in which we live, the facts of which are available to all of us.

Is it a good world then?

People disagree about it.

There are attitudes corresponding to the judgements we made about the nature of the universe. These range from joyful acceptance to despair; from acquiescence to rebellion. The same world gives rise to different judgements and to different attitudes. The same world is experienced in different ways. It's the 'even though...after all' applied in different ways again! Not only by different people, but by the same person. For, at some times we are impressed with the irrationality of it all. At other times we feel that we begin to see a purpose and are willing to accept it with equanimity, and believe that good will come out of it, even if at

Religion and Science

present we do not see all things as evidence of love or loving purpose.

In the last analysis, it is a matter of decision, of choice and of resolve. But, as we have insisted, the taking of a believing attitude (like the taking of an unbelieving or an agnostic attitude) need not be arbitrary. We can specify the features of a reasonable attitude and decision and thus differentiate it from an arbitrary one.

A reasonable attitude is, first, one for which we can give reasons with a view to producing a rational conviction. Our assumption is that that for which we can give acceptable reasons is worthy of attention and credance in preference to that for which no such reasons can be given.

Second, we can point to facts in the world which such an attitude illuminates and explain how it illuminates such facts. Such facts will be of different kinds, some of a personal, some of an impersonal, some of a social character. Since the facts are diverse, the illumination will be of different kinds.

Third, we can show how such 'faith' provides integration for the whole person. It does not simply explain the world in an abstract and intellectual fashion. It has to do with life as it is lived within the world by man who is a feeling and volitional as well as an intellectual being.

But, when all is said, we rest the case.

We say that the pattern we see in the world is somehow explained by the claim we are making about it. We experience the world (=everything that is to be experienced) in a particular way. Since we are taking up an attitude to 'everything' we are not now concerned about establishing the facts but of connections between them and how such connections are to be made. Our concern is about experiences which when seen as significant enable us to make such constructive and illuminating connections. The world can be seen in *this* way. It can be seen in *that* way. Since it is the world, i.e. everything, to which we are taking an attitude everything must be illuminated, must be seen to fit and not be explained away. We should not at some point have to put on the blinkers so that we will not be distracted by disturbing facts. Otherwise we shall not be facing reality, and be open to the diagnosis of neurosis. The pattern we discern within the totality enables us to see and not to close our eyes to the facts.

The Pattern of the World

The discernment of the pattern is conviction-producing. We make out a convincing case which is not arbitrary. But, in the end, as with *any* fundamental attitude we rest the case. The procedure is analogous to what happens in court. When the facts are 'in', it is then a matter of persuasion by a process of discussion, a bringing of reasons and arguments so that it can be 'seen' that the perspective is correct and—let's say—the accused is innocent. When all the facts have been presented, and the arguments have been stated, it is then a matter of 'resting the case', in the assurance that a fair statement of matters which has produced conviction for you will be likely to produce conviction to your hearers. It is an appeal to 'satisfaction'. A valid appeal to satisfacion can only occur when it takes the path of reason.

In illustration let us take some possible situations from family life, where sometimes people are asked to give explanations of states of affairs around the house. 'Why is dinner late today?' 'Where is Ronald?' 'What happened to the £5 note I left on the desk?' 'Why haven't the gas men come again?'

In each of these situations there are certain answers we would accept as reasonable, rest our case and then pass from the question and go on to other matters. We would rest the case because we had been satisfied. So with the late dinner, 'I've been spring cleaning and forgot the time' would be fair. 'The bus was late and so I couldn't help it' would perhaps be even better. But, 'I thought it was tomorrow, when you don't come home to dinner', would strike one as being rather poor. We happily rest the case where the best reason was given.

About the £5. To say, 'The dog ran off with it' strikes one as being, at the best, evasive, perhaps facetious. 'You don't think I'm satisfied with that tale do you?' So your wife comes in and says, 'Oh, the £5? Well, you know, I thought it was mine'. You answer, resigned, but hardly satisfied, 'But you should have known better than that'. A better answer would be, 'I needed it to pay the milk bill, so I borrowed it'.

As to the gas men. You would probably be told something along these lines: 'You know what they are like. They never come when you want them and when they come you're either not in, or they bring the wrong things or find they've come about a quite different job.' The idea being conveyed is that you have to accept the sort of thing you're asking questions about, without asking questions. You are supposed to respond, 'Oh yes, that's true, isn't it?' So, accepting it as a working principle that this is the condition of affairs, based upon your own experience and the experience of people you have known, you (wearily) rest the case.

In each of these examples we would, in short, rest the case because we had been satisfied, when the reasonable explanation had been given.

There are other instances where we would find it more difficult. For example, suppose someone asked, 'Why does this house have to be like a circus at the week-end?' we would I suppose in the end rest satisfied (assuming we accepted the terms of the question and its legitimacy) with the best reasons we were given, even if they left some loose ends. 'Well, it's good for the young people. They like to have friends in and play games and records. They're better off here than somewhere else. Besides, you don't really mind, do you?'

If there were a better and a worse explanation we would only rest satisfied with the better explanation. But, and it is an important 'but', the very fact that a reasonable person rests satisfied with an explanation would mean that (at least for him) that explanation was the better one, that it provided satisfaction for him, that he could take his stand on it. There he would rest his case.

'Resting the case' about the world means taking a fundamental attitude to it, moving from a perspective, thinking, acting and experiencing in the light of a perspective and maintaining and extending the satisfaction which such a perspective provides.

The Christian believer includes God in his perspective, and finds it illuminating to claim that God is love, and that the world is his creation.

Summary and Conclusion

When we try to find a pattern in the world we have different kinds of facts to account for. Whether we say that the world is irrational or rational we shall be taking a fundamental attitude to the facts. This involves us in making a decision, since it is not a wholly intellectual matter. The believer wishes to give reasons for his attitude, thus showing it to be reasonable. Having done this he then rests the case, believing that if given a hearing it will produce the kind of satisfaction it has for him.

Discussion Questions

Upon what facts within the world would you base a judgement about what the world is like? Would you accept certain facts as more significant than others in making such a judgement?

Would you consider your attitude to other races, other classes reasonable? Is this because you have already given reasons to yourself? What reasons could be given for such attitudes?

Are there attitudes which you would accept without further discussion? If so, why?

The Christian believer says that the life, death and resurrection of Jesus Christ provides the clue to the meaning of the world, and takes his attitude from that. Would you consider this reasonable? Why or why not?

For further reading the following sources are suggested

Ian Barbour, *Science and Religion*, London, S.C.M. Press, 1968.
Langdon Gilkey, *Religion and the Scientific Future*, London, S.C.M. Press, 1970.
Paul Tillich, *Dynamics of Faith*, London, Allen and Unwin, 1957.

The source of the parable of the Stranger is:
Basil Mitchell, 'Theology and Falsification' in *New Essays in Philosophical Theology*, edited by Antony Flew and Alasdair MacIntyre, London, S.C.M. Press, 1961.

INDEX

Aristotle, 33
Arrhenius, 43
Atheism, 79

Belief, 73, 113-5
Brecht, Bertold, 33
Buddha, Buddhism, 55

Christian history, 110f
Christianity, 57
Concern, 74, 93, 99
Conflict, resolution of, 17
Control, 87ff
Copernicus, 18
creatio ex nihilo, 110,111

Defining 'religion', 69ff

Explanation, levels of, 10, 60

Facts and evidence, 40ff
Facts and theory, 35-37
Faith, 112ff

Generalisations, 70ff
Galileo, 33
God, talk about, 59
Gotama, 55

Hamlet, 10
History, 110

Islam, 56, 92

Judaism, 92, 97, 98

Kant, Immanuel, 23, 38

Laplace, 29
Law, scientific, 25, 35
Liberal, 82f
Linnaeus, Carl, 81
Luther, Martin, 18

Mechanism, 81
Miracles, 53ff
Mohammed, 56
Moses, 59
Myth, mythical, mythological 101

Neptune, discovery of, 25
Nobel, Alfred, 85
Nonsense, 63ff

Oppenheimer, J. Robert, 86

Ptolemy, 19

Religion, defining, 69ff
Regularity, 25-6
'Resting the case', 124-5
Religious concern
  for the future, 93,99
Religious symbols, 94
Resurrection, 56-58
Revelation, 106ff

Index

Scientific method, 32-37
Secularization, 81
Sense experience, 64
Sherlock Holmes, 41
Syllogism, 27ff.
Symbols (religious), 94-96
Theology, 107
Theory, 33ff
Two compartments, 83
Traditionalist, 82f

World, 122ff

Zen Buddhism, 66
Zoroastrianism, 53-4

www.ingramcontent.com/pod-product-compliance
Lightning Source LLC
LaVergne TN
LVHW041225080426
835508LV00011B/1090